The
Sheltering
Branch

The Sheltering Branch

Marzieh Gail, M.A.

BAHÁ'Í
PUBLISHING

WILMETTE, ILLINOIS

Bahá'í Publishing
401 Greenleaf Avenue, Wilmette, Illinois 60091

Copyright © 1959, Marzieh Gail

All rights reserved. Published 2021

Printed in the United States of America on acid-free paper ∞

24   23   22   21   4   3   2   1

The Sheltering Branch was first published by George Ronald
(Oxford, UK) in 1959. The first US edition of the work was
published by the Bahá'í Publishing Trust of the United States
in 1970. This revised edition was prepared for publication in
2021 to mark the centenary of the passing of 'Abdu'l-Bahá.

ISBN 978-1-61851-206-2

Cover photograph by Sholeh Samadani Munion
Book and cover design by Patrick Falso

". . . this Branch of Holiness;
well is it with him that hath sought His shelter
and abideth beneath His shadow."

—*Bahá'u'lláh*

Contents

Preface to the Centenary Edition

It is with great pleasure that the US Bahá'í Publishing Trust presents this revised edition of *The Sheltering Branch* in honor of the centenary of the passing of 'Abdu'l-Bahá. Its author, Marzieh Gail, was one of the great Bahá'í writers, and in this slim volume she offers a beautiful and moving tribute to the life and teachings of the Master. In preparing this edition, small editorial changes have been made for the sake of clarity and to provide updated translations of some of the passages quoted; however, great care has been taken to preserve the integrity of the original book, first published in 1959.

It should be noted that passages taken from the memoirs of the author's mother, Mrs. Florence Breed Khan (referred to herein as Florence Khánum), fall into the category of pilgrims' notes. These passages, which describe the words and actions of 'Abdu'l-Bahá, should be considered the recollections of the author, and not as authoritative accounts of the words and deeds of the Master.

The Unity of
East and West

A member of the Académie Française is reported as saying that the most interesting life of the nineteenth century was Benjamin Disraeli's. This statement reminds us, if we need to be reminded again, that even to European intellectuals the nineteenth is still the unknown century. At a certain point in time two thousand years ago there was only one pivotal fact in the world: the life of Christ. And the nineteenth century in its turn, saw only one pivotal fact: the intertwined lives of the Báb and Bahá'u'lláh; the life and martyrdom of the Báb, and then, *"after the lapse of a few years,"* the *"Beauty of the Báb . . . arrayed in a new raiment . . ."*[1]

As another aspect of this central fact, the nineteenth century saw the birth, and the first fifty-six years of the life of 'Abdu'l-Bahá; of Him Who "forms together with them . . . the Three Central Figures of a Faith that stands unapproached in the world's spiritual history."[2] For the

1

Father, in the nineteenth century, brought down the bread from heaven once again; and it is man himself who has preferred a stone.

To study a man's life is to live in his presence, through his words and the words of those who saw him or who have thought about him; and especially it is to see him in the lives of those he has influenced. Now that His pen is stilled, His voice hushed, 'Abdu'l-Bahá's words are the Bahá'ís; they are His message to the world; His conversation with mankind; and they reflect, however tentatively at this early stage of apprenticeship in Bahá'í living, the life of 'Abdu'l-Bahá—of Him Who is *"the Master," "the Centre of the Covenant," "the Mystery of God," "the Limb of the Law of God," "the Interpreter"* of the mind of Bahá'u'lláh, *"the Architect of His World Order," "the Exemplar of His faith,"* and *"the Ensign of His Most Great Peace."*[3]

After Bahá'u'lláh ascended, a prisoner and exile, near 'Akká in 1892, a telegram was sent to the Sultan whose prisoner He was. It read: "The Sun of Bahá has set." 'Abdu'l-Bahá was left then, almost alone in the world, to face the enemies who were massed against Him—enemies from within and without the Cause, some His own blood relatives, others as close at hand, others in faraway countries where renown of this Faith had even then penetrated.

Even before Bahá'u'lláh had declared His mission in 1863, 'Abdu'l-Bahá, as a child of eight, had recognized His Father's station and had thrown Himself down and asked to die for His sake. Bahá'u'lláh addressed Him:

O Thou Who art the apple of Mine eye![4]

and wrote:

We have made Thee a shelter for all mankind, a shield unto all who are in heaven and on earth, a stronghold for whosoever hath believed in God, the Incomparable, the All-Knowing.[5]

And once when 'Abdu'l-Bahá was on a visit to Beirut, Bahá'u'lláh in 'Akká, said of His departure:

Sorrow, thereby, hath enveloped this Prison-city, whilst another land rejoiceth. . . . Blessed, doubly blessed, is the ground which His footsteps have trodden, the eye that hath been cheered by the beauty of His countenance, the ear that hath been honoured by hearkening to His call, the heart that hath tasted the sweetness of His love, the breast that hath dilated through His remembrance, the pen that hath voiced His praise, the scroll that hath borne the testimony of His writings.[6]

He was the beautiful, the brilliant, the adoring eldest Son to Whom Bahá'u'lláh, in His Will, entrusted His Faith; Whom He singled out for honors and blessings on account of His sheer merit—and Whose perfections aroused, Shoghi Effendi tells us, an envy as deadly as that of Joseph's brothers, as deep as that in the heart of Cain.[7]

The Muslims have a holy tradition to the effect that in the latter days, the sun will rise in the West. It was 'Abdu'l-Bahá Who, in the black time after His Father left Him, directed His thoughts westward and began to focus the light of the Faith on North America. The result was that sixty years after the ascension of Bahá'u'lláh, the Guardian of the Cause could draw a map tracing the development of the newly-launched ten-year Bahá'í crusade for the spiritual conquest of the planet; and this map, which shows the directional movements of the crusade, features great rays radiating out across the world from North America. For a remarkable thing had taken place; there had been a swing outward from Persia, where the light of God first struck, and (to borrow from Fitzgerald's phrase) a noose of light had caught the towers of the West; a mysterious agency had linked Chicago and Shíráz.

"The establishment of the Faith of Bahá'u'lláh in the Western Hemisphere," was, the Guardian writes, "the most outstanding achievement that will forever be associated with 'Abdu'l-Bahá's ministry. . . ."[8]

The Báb and Bahá'u'lláh had been Prisoners. "For the first time since the inception of the Faith, sixty–six years previously, its Head and supreme Representative burst asunder the shackles, . . . "[9] the Guardian tells us, saying too that the Master's three years of travel (to Egypt, Europe, and America):

4

mark . . . a turning point of the utmost significance in the history of the century.

'Abdu'l-Bahá was at this time broken in health. He suffered from several maladies brought on by the strains and stresses of a tragic life spent almost wholly in exile and imprisonment. He was on the threshold of three-score years and ten. Yet as soon as He was released from His forty-year long captivity, as soon as He had laid the Báb's body in a safe and permanent resting-place, and His mind was free of grievous anxieties connected with the execution of that priceless Trust, He arose with sublime courage, confidence and resolution to consecrate what little strength remained to Him, in the evening of His life, to a service of such heroic proportions that no parallel to it is to be found in the annals of the first Bahá'í century. . . .

Inflexibly resolved to undertake this arduous voyage, at whatever cost to His strength, at whatever risk to His life, He, quietly and without any previous warning, on a September afternoon, of the year 1910, . . . sailed for Egypt. . . .[10]

The first time that the Master set out for the West, He had to abandon the voyage. He had remained about a month in Port Said, "and from thence embarked with the intention of proceeding to Europe, only to discover that the condition of His health necessitated His landing again at Alexandria and postponing His voyage."[11] And these Western journeys "called forth," the Guardian further says, "the last ounce of His ebbing strength. . . ."[12]

Perhaps this is one reason why, when very old and ailing believers arise in these days to leave their homes and emigrate for the Cause, the Guardian encourages their going. Certainly this exodus of young and old from their countries is an echo of the travels of 'Abdu'l-Bahá. This mass pioneer movement of Bahá'ís, in respect of the distances traversed and the complexity of the problems faced, has no precedent in history. Thousands of Bahá'í families and individuals have left their homes, not for war or pilgrimage or travel, not as fugitives, not as an employment or to seek their health or fortune, but for the sole sake of spreading Bahá'u'lláh's Cause around the world. Such journeys, however arduous, bring a special consolation to those privileged to take part in them; the Master compares them to the departures of the disciples of Christ . . . God says in the Qur'án: "And they who have fled their country and quitted their homes and suffered in My Cause, and have fought and fallen, I will blot out their sins from them, and I will bring them into gardens beneath which the streams do flow. . . . They shall abide therein forever."[13]

'Abdu'l-Bahá traveled through the United States (and to Canada) for nine months, sowing a harvest so vast that time will never be able to gather it all. In a published letter, He is reported as saying of these travels that He had *"breathed on the souls and spirits of all the Bahá'ís in such a way that had it been upon bone, it would have taken on flesh. . . ."*[14] And America became the "cradle of the Administrative Order,"[15] as Persia is the cradle of the Faith; of that Administrative Order which is "the nucleus [and] very pattern of the New World Order,"[16] so that 'Abdu'l-Bahá's Will and Testament, proclaiming and formally establishing the Administrative Order,[17] is at the same time the "Charter of a future world civilization."[18]

In Bahá'í history, then, Persia and America are indissolubly linked; "the seed of the Divinely-appointed Administration" lay, the Guardian writes, "In the blood of the unnumbered martyrs of Persia."[19] 'Abdu'l-Bahá desired *"a perfect bond between Persia and America. . . ."*[20] He told the Orient-Occident Unity Conference in Washington:

> For the Persians there is no government better fitted to contribute to the development of their natural resources and the helping of their national needs in a reciprocal alliance than the United States of America, and for the Americans there could be no better industrial outlet and market than . . . Persia. The mineral wealth of Persia is still latent and untouched. It is my hope that the great American democracy may be instrumental in developing these hidden resources. . . . May the material civilization of America find complete efficacy and establishment

in Persia, and may the spiritual civilization of Persia find acceptance and response in America.[21]

From such a connection, He said, there would be *"great harvests of results."* [22] He prophesied that the time would come when the East and the West would embrace *"like unto two lovers."* [23]

The Manuscript of Florence Khánum

In the days when 'Abdu'l-Bahá was still a prisoner in 'Akká, a young Bahá'í woman, nursing her first baby, left New England with husband and child and went on a pilgrimage to see Him. She was the first American Bahá'í to marry a Persian, and the Master had written, *"This is the first conjugal union between East and West."* He had named her little son Raḥím (the youngest pilgrim who had come to Him from the Occident), *"the first fruits of the spiritual union between East and West."* Half a century has now gone by since that pilgrimage. The young woman grew old and died, and when her papers were opened the manuscript was found of a book that she had written, called *Wanderers* (taking this title from the marriage Tablet revealed for her husband and herself by the Master which said: *"They are wanderers in Thy domain, and enamoured of Thy beauty.* ")[1] Some sections of this manuscript will be given here; the account has only the status of all other pilgrims' reports, but it helps to recapture a time long gone (as human lives are measured), and it gives an impression of the Master as seen through Western eyes, and focuses attention on this central theme of His ministry: the unity of East and West. The writer's name was Florence Breed. She was called Florence Khánum. I knew her very well; she was my mother.

Fifty years ago the average young American gentlewoman did not venture far into the East; and if there, she went gingerly, carefully insulated. Florence begins by describing her first visit to Constantinople, where her own mother had taken her on what was known as the Grand Tour. She then proceeds to contrast this with her second visit to the Turkish capital, on her way to 'Akká as the wife of a Persian Bahá'í:

> On my first visit to Constantinople as a girl of seventeen with my dear mother and younger sister Alice, when we visited the Stamboul bazaars Mother always cautioned us upon entering the dim, arched interior, "Turn right, to the European bazaar, where we shall be perfectly safe. . . ." I remember how we walked demurely along following our dear mother—and how the Eastern merchants seeing apparently 'rich Americans' strolling by, rushed out of their "bou-

tiques" with articles in their hands, vociferously imploring us to buy—following us with pleadings, until our mother's final decisive "No's!" dismissed them in the end.

So when Khán* said, "Today we lunch with the jewelers to the Sultan, they are Bahá'ís," and I asked, "Where is the luncheon?" and he replied, "We go into the bazaars to their office," I recalled the earlier visit in my girlhood. Arriving at the bazaars we entered, and instead of turning right towards the prosperous-looking, better-lighted, European section, we turned left and walked into the dimmer less-frequented "Oriental" bazaar. Following my husband (who was wearing a Turkish fez to facilitate our movements in Turkey), and with some trepidation of heart, I recalled my dear mother's warning, which hardly allowed our glances to look at the Oriental section, and here was her daughter not only actually penetrating those dim corridors, going towards an unknown, Eastern goal, but going as the wife of an Easterner!

"Kismet!" I murmured to myself. "Destiny! What am I adventuring into? However, so far, so good. And it is undeniable I dearly love and trust my hus-

---

* 'Alí-Kuli Khán, Nabíl-i-Dawlih, Florence's husband, the author's father. Qulí (Kuli) means "son of."

band. So here goes!" On we went, hardly meeting anyone, and turned into a vast open courtyard, also nearly deserted. My husband, with our son, led the way to some steps, going down into a kind of cellar. Here came forward the Bahá'í brothers hospitably greeting all three of us as warmly as long lost, old, dear friends. We were at once comfortably installed in the pleasant, underground room, and a servant appeared, bearing goblets of delectable, cool Persian sherbet, most welcome after our warm walk. . . . In such kindness, and perfect atmosphere of loving brotherhood, all strangeness disappeared. I felt completely safe. . . . "What a Faith!" I thought, "that can unite East and West! That can make an American feel at one, in spiritual sympathy, with an Easterner. Indeed, the Bahá'í Revelation is a key to unlock hearts, to unite in fellowship and understanding the people of the world, whatever the race, whatever the spiritual background!"

So, little by little, I was learning to modify my ignorances and prejudices of the West—that burden of inheritance that the people of Europe and America are born into, without realizing it, ever since the Middle Ages!

The Master in 'Akká

It should not be surprising that the offer, with kindness, of a cool drink should help to change a Westerner's long-established attitudes. World peace will be founded on small actions within the reach of everyone, and given such actions no charts or scholarly treatises to prove the oneness of mankind, or to solve the economic question, are necessary. "Tender, loving care," as Western psychologists now say, is the only prerequisite. Those who think that by love for humanity is meant an academic abstraction, who "love humanity" but not one human being, have never studied 'Abdu'l-Bahá. The love He teaches is nothing else than the service embodied in His name, 'Abd—Servant. *"He who serves (mankind) has already entered the Kingdom and is seated at the right hand of his Lord."* [1] He says that Bahá'ís must be as kind to people as God is:

We must consider none bad, none worthy of detestation, no one as an enemy. . . . Bahá'u'lláh has clearly said . . . that if you have an enemy, consider him not as an enemy. Do not simply be long-suffering; nay, rather, love him. Your treatment of him should be that which is becoming to lovers. Do not even say that he is your enemy. Do not see any enemies. Though he be your murderer, see no enemy. Look upon him with the eye of friendship. Be mindful that you do not consider him as an enemy and simply tolerate him, for that is but stratagem and hypocrisy. To consider a man your enemy and love him is hypocrisy.[2]

The present writer, after many years of thinking over this statement (which in Christianity has remained only a counsel of perfection for twenty centuries) has come to understand it in terms of a statement attributed in the East to Plato: that Heaven is a bow, and events are arrows; man is the target, and God the archer. . . . The event is, it would seem then, to be loved, because it comes from the Archer. In any case, if mankind will relinquish its hatreds and deliberately substitute love—the love which results from the performance of loving acts—'Abdu'l-Bahá offers this spectacular promise:

If you attain to such a capacity of love and unity, the Blessed Perfection will shower infinite graces of the spiritual Kingdom upon you, guide, protect and preserve you under the shadow of His Word, increase your happiness in this world and uphold you through all difficulties.[3]

Non-personal only in the sense of being impartially distributed, the Master's was a warm mother-love; each one felt that 'Abdu'l-Bahá's love was especially for him, just as each one appropriates his own place in the sun. This is how Florence Khánum describes the first time she saw the Master:

With what a thrill of the spirit, with what gratified joy of the heart I silently mounted that long flight of stone steps—nearer and nearer to the Heaven of 'Abdu'l-Bahá's presence! At the top, we were led to the right, through a little stone vestibule into a long and bare living-room, with many windows overlooking the sunshine and color of the blue Mediterranean. A divan, Eastern fashion, ran along all the walls.

The Master stood by the window facing our entrance. Khán in extreme emotion advanced ahead to the Master, Whose loving arms encircled him as they embraced, and Whose strengthening, cheery, encouraging voice cried out in great heartiness, *"Marḥabá! Marḥabá! Welcome! Well done! Well done!"* Khán, half weeping, and trembling in excessive love and joy, overcome with the Master's welcome and praise, brought Raḥím and me forward. "My wife and son!" Again came the glorious words, *"Marḥabá! Marḥabá! You went one to America, Khán, and you return three!"*

Many people were overcome in the Master's presence, because the impact of His perfection was too hard to bear. As the days passed, Florence was able more calmly to contemplate this Being, Whom she calls the "Archetypal Man of the great Bahá'í Era." At His table, where she, the only woman present, sat beside Him at luncheon and dinner almost without exception (once He entertained official guests in a big white tent, and again served two hundred people on His birthday, so that the regular meals were interrupted) during her thirty-three days' visit, she watched and listened; when He addressed her, Alí-Kuli Khán translated in a low voice.

As I gazed at Him, I became aware of a kind of spiritual vision. He seemed to be deeply breathing the airs of an upper ether, to be inhaling the Breath of Life from a source and an atmosphere far, far above the ken of men and angels. From a world higher than our world and superior to it . . . [He is] in our world, in a lower, an alien element, but draws His breath, life and sustenance from the Higher Spheres.

. . . In studying 'Abdu'l-Bahá in the first day or two (for after I had discerned His perfections there was no more attempt to "study" Him) I could only gaze at Him in shyness and in awe. . . . 'Abdu'l-Bahá wore a snowy-white scarf wound about a *café-au-lait* soft, tassel-less kind of fez. Over His white, long overdress, He wore a thin *'abá,* sometimes a *dust-'abá,* of black or brown thin material, oftener one of *café-au-lait* color. In the snowy scarf about His waist, I saw a pink rose occasionally tucked, and on a devastatingly hot midsummer noon, I was surprised to see the rose as fresh and dewy-looking as if it were the dawn.

At times, the prized, first odor of the East emanates from Him—attar of roses—while there is ever a spiritual radiance and fragrance which one perceives spiritually and which uplifts one's inner being and . . . brings one into the "garden of Abhá."

She tells of walking through the soft Eastern night, going across the courtyard under the big white stars, on her way to the evening meal, and saying to herself,

"I am on my way . . . and who am I? to take dinner with the Divine Host of the world!" . . . Upon entering the hall, we stood about awaiting the arrival of the Master. Never was this "Rose of the World" alone! Always accompanying Him were a number of faithful Eastern Bahá'í men, in the dress of their respective countries—wearing the red fez, the black kuláh, the white turban.

She tells of seeing the Master in the bright moonlight:

[He] raised His beloved face, and gazed upward lingeringly at the glory of the full moon. I can never forget those moments of beauty—the moon, a masterpiece of God, shining in full glory in the high heavens, being admiringly looked upon by a, masterpiece of God on earth: 'Abdu'l-Bahá!

One night she had a strange, subjective experience:

One evening, after sunset, Khán came in great enthusiasm and excitement to our room. "Do you remember," he asked, "that 'Abdu'l-Bahá said He would answer all the letters we brought to Him from America before we left?" "Yes, I do." "Then come quickly. It is too wonderful! The Master is pacing to and fro, in His sitting room—I cannot see the secretary—and He is replying to those letters, as if He had known the inmost secret of the writers' hearts, from the cradle! Yet He has never met nor seen one of them. You can see Him from the corridor beyond the little room, each time He passes the open door-

way!" So, Raḥím being peacefully asleep, I returned
with <u>Kh</u>án, to his post, outside the doorway which
led to 'Abdu'l-Bahá's long room with its many windows looking over the Bay of 'Akká to the Mediterranean beyond. I heard the dear Master's beautiful voice, and then saw Him, as He strode by the
doorway of His lighted room. We were in the dark,
looking through the small darkened antechamber. I
recalled how, never, at the daily luncheon table, and
never at the late evening dinner, and never at any
time, had I satisfied my longing to gaze more fully
upon the Master's beautiful, noble and spiritual
face. I used to glance admiringly at the snowy, scarf-
enfolded headdress, and at the beautiful, silver-white
hair falling softly to the shoulders; and at the lofty
arch of His forehead, at the expression of His eyes,
indescribable in human language; now they seemed
blue—and now brown—and again partly of each
color, or hazel—but always illumined, loving and
understanding; sometimes raised in holy reverence,
in silent prayer, sometimes gently smiling—but
always kingly and supreme. . . . Then, I could never
get my fill, so to speak, of the divine beauty of the
lower part of His face. It expressed only a perfect
sweetness, a heavenly, Divine perfection of spiri-
tuality—a gentleness—a holy patience—no sign
whatsoever in lines or expression of the lower traits

of human nature, only a Divine perfectness. It was astounding. I had never seen a face like it. Selfless. The stamp of suffering upon it; alas for humanity, which crucifies God's messengers!*

So, I thought exultingly, "Now if only the Master would pause a moment in His doorway, as I am here in the dark, I could look upon His face to my heart's content, and no one would notice me!"

Instantly, the Master stopped in His doorway. Silhouetted against the light, I clearly saw Him in His beauty, and I began a sort of "visual devouring" of that wonderful face! I looked, and I looked, and I looked. After a few moments, 'Abdu'l-Bahá withdrew, and resumed His pacing to and fro and revelation of the Tablets.

After watching for a while, half timorously the thought arose in my heart, "Oh! if only He would stop once more in the doorway!"

At once the Master stood in the doorway, silent, and seemed to be looking upwards towards the stars. "Now, I *will* look!" I thought in breathless joy.

This time as I gazed silently upon that matchless face, a golden light shone forth from His entire

---

* Florence K͟hánum is not implying that the Master was a Prophet. ". . . 'Abdu'l-Bahá is not a Manifestation of God . . . though the successor of His Father, He does not occupy a cognate station. . . ." (Shoghi Effendi, *The World Order of Bahá'u'lláh,* p. 132) M.G.

figure. This light intensified, and intensified, as I looked, and looked, until I began almost to be afraid.

I said to myself, "However bright it grows I am going to keep my eyes open! What a wonderful sight! What a miraculous opportunity!"

The outline of light grew more and more intense, yet I looked, and I looked, until it seemed to me, I must fall upon my knees. Just as it seemed I could no longer bear such a vision, the Master withdrew.

"Take me to my room," I said weakly, much overcome, to Khán. "I have just seen the transfiguration upon the Mount!"

Later I asked Khán if he had seen anything unusual. "No," he replied. "I noticed that the Master stopped twice in the doorway, and that He looked very beautiful. That was all."

Then he advised me that whatever I saw, of the miraculous, at 'Akká, I had best not teach it in America. "A Bahá'í is not supposed to teach by relating the miraculous, if it come within his experience," he said. "Because his listener has not seen it, and much as he may believe the person who has, it may convey nothing to him."

This scene of the Tablets reminds us that almost without interruption, ever since 1844, thousands of Tablets, and in our times of the Guardian's letters, have been showered on the world. By the mass of mankind unnoticed as the air, many of these are general epistles to society, while others are highly personal, so that many an individual life has been founded on one or another of them. In this connection the writer cannot help remembering how a well-known Christian evangelist, current model, answers his mail. According to the magazine *Match* (8 June 1957), this man receives from ten to fifteen thousand letters a week. In a locked room, seven young women, working at top speed, open these letters, quantities of which contain money gifts, and all of which ask for advice. The letters are then read by eight secretaries, who, using different-colored pencils, underline the key words. The words thus underlined determine the answer which the seeker of advice is going to receive, since, in the majority of cases, the answer is composed by a robot typewriter in which has been placed a key corresponding to one of some forty principal letter-topics: unbelieving husband, segregation, atomic tests, recent conversion, baptism, military service, etc. It is certainly appropriate that in our age of mechanization human beings should, in their desperate hours, turn for solace to a machine.

The Attainable
Perfections of Man

For our present purposes we shall define 'Abdu'l-Bahá's message as the affirmation of the perfectibility of man. *"The greatest bestowal of God to man,"* He says, *"is the capacity to attain human virtues."*[1] And elsewhere: *"The purpose of the creation of man is the attainment of the supreme virtues of humanity through descent of the heavenly bestowals."*[2] The goal He sets is the *"happiness of humanity"* to be achieved by man's accumulated perfections, as these are realized by man's own unceasing effort. In His farewell to a group of Bahá'ís He told them:

> This is our last evening and I ask God that His confirmations may encompass you. . . . May you all be united, may you be agreed, may you serve the solidarity of mankind. May you be well-wishers of

all humanity. May you be assistants of every poor one. May you be nurses for the sick. May you be sources of comfort to the broken in heart. May you be a refuge for the wanderer. May you be a source of courage to the affrighted one. Thus, through the favor and assistance of God may the standard of the happiness of humanity be held aloft in the center of the world. . . .[3]

When facing the mystery of any human being, even of this "Mystery of God," 'Abdu'l-Bahá, one key to his nature is the words or expressions that he often repeats. With the Master, one finds, over and over, such words as "Arise, go forth, strive, advance, become, attain." Choosing at random the first thirty-five pages of the book *The Promulgation of Universal Peace* ('Abdu'l-Bahá's talks during His nine-months'-long journeys in North America) one finds that, while it is not possible to make an exact, objective count, ideas connected with these words and their synonyms occur at least one hundred and twenty-five times. *Arise, go forth, strive, advance, become, attain.*

Humanity today has lived through two world wars. Adults living today have been forced to look on scenes of horror that they can never forget. Their hearts have been disfigured by grief. Avidly enjoying a few years of respite now, many of them are pursuing the things of this world as relentlessly as those unscathed materialists in the so-far-untouched sections of the globe. When approached by a Bahá'í their comment is: "You can't change human nature." An astronomical number of times, when you talk to the average man, you get some such answer as: "I'm only the little fellow. It's the big fellows who make the wars. Nothing I do can change anything." They answer in this way first out of despair, then as a convenient rationalization of their chosen way of life, but fundamentally because they do not know what man is.

This modern phenomenon of despair, which has made suicide so common in our times that every high bridge and building must have some structural provision against it, is in Islamic prophecy one of the signs of the Day of Resurrection; Muḥammad foretold that on that Day a man, passing by another's grave, would say: "Would to God I were in his place" (Sale, *Preliminary Discourse*).

Against this universal phenomenon of despair, speaks out 'Abdu'l-Bahá. The Manifestations of God, He says, are sent *"to uplift the human race from the abyss of despair . . ."*[4] and again, *"they liberate man from the darkness of the world of nature, deliver him from despair. . . ."*[5]

One of His prayers says:

In the darksome night of despair, my eye turneth expectant and full of hope to the morn of Thy boundless favor and at the hour of dawn my drooping soul is refreshed and strengthened in remembrance of Thy beauty and perfection. He whom the grace of Thy mercy aideth, though he be but a drop, shall become the boundless ocean, and the merest atom which the outpouring of Thy loving-kindness assisteth, shall shine even as the radiant star.[6]

This theme is also stated in the only recording we have of 'Abdu'l-Bahá's voice.*

Modern man belittles himself and fritters away his days because he does not know what he is. To awaken him before his moment in the light is gone forever, the Master echoes around the world His Father's statement on the power of one righteous act:

One righteous act is endowed with a potency that can so elevate the dust as to cause it to pass beyond the heaven of heavens. It can tear every bond asunder, and hath the power to restore the force that hath spent itself and vanished. . . .[7]

He urges man to read the Hidden Words, where Bahá'u'lláh says to humanity:

---

* Since this [book] was written, a double-sided recording of 'Abdu'l-Bahá's voice has come to light, one side in Persian, the other in Turkish. Mr Rustom Sabit informs us that through the good offices of his father, this recording was made by Pathé of Paris. Copies are preserved in the Bahá'í International Archives at Haifa.

Thou art even as a finely tempered sword concealed in the darkness of its sheath and its value hidden from the artificer's knowledge. Wherefore come forth from the sheath of self and desire that thy worth may be made resplendent and manifest unto all the world.[8]

To prove man's perfectibility, 'Abdu'l-Bahá explains what man is, and where man stands in relation to man, to the world, and to the Lord of the world. Man, He says, is the world-tree's fruit;[9] man is to the world what the spirit is to the body,[10] what the head is to the human form:

So if we were to imagine a time when man belonged to the animal kingdom, that is, when he was merely an animal, existence would have been imperfect. This means that there would have been no man, and this chief member, which in the body of the world is like the mind and the brain in a human being, would have been lacking. . . . for man is the chief member of the body of this world, and a body without its chief member is undoubtedly imperfect.[11]

He is the vital life of the world, and present-day man in his foredoomed attempts to compete with the animal, to burrow down and hide in the animal kingdom, is depriving this world of its quintessential life.

Man is the life of the world, and the life of man is the spirit. The happiness of the world depends upon man, and the happiness of man is dependent upon the spirit.[12]

As He glances around the world, assigning to each phenomenon its rank and place, the Master has much to say of the five divisions of the spirit:

The greatest power in the realm and range of human existence is spirit—the divine breath which animates and pervades all things. It is manifested throughout creation in different degrees or kingdoms. In the vegetable kingdom it is the . . . power of growth. . . . In this degree of its manifestation[,] spirit is unconscious of the powers which qualify the kingdom of the animal. The distinctive virtue or plus of the animal is sense perception; it sees, hears, smells, tastes and feels but is incapable, in turn, of conscious ideation or reflection which characterizes and differentiates the human kingdom. . . . From the visible it cannot draw conclusions regarding the invisible . . . this power is a distinctive attribute of the human spirit. . . . The animal spirit cannot penetrate and discover the mysteries of things. It is a captive of the senses. No amount of teaching, for instance, would enable it to grasp the fact that the sun is stationary, and the earth moves around it. Likewise, the human spirit has its limitations. It cannot comprehend the phenomena of the Kingdom transcending the human station, for it is a captive of powers and life forces which have their operation upon its own plane of existence, and it cannot go beyond that boundary.

There is, however, another Spirit, which may be termed the Divine, to which Jesus Christ refers when He declares that man must be born of its quickening and baptized with its living fire. Souls deprived of that Spirit are accounted as dead, though they are possessed of the human spirit. Jesus Christ . . . means that souls, though alive in the human kingdom, are nevertheless dead if devoid of this particular spirit of divine quickening. They have not partaken of the divine life of the higher Kingdom. . . .[13]

This last, the *"spirit of faith,"* is spirit in the fourth degree;[14] it is the light reflected back from the believing heart. And spirit in the fifth degree is the Holy Spirit, *". . . the effulgent rays that emanate from His Manifestation. . . ."*[15] Spirit in the fourth degree is *that power which makes the earthly soul heavenly and the imperfect man perfect. It cleanses the impure, unlooses the tongue of the silent . . . and confers knowledge upon the ignorant."*[16] Without the fifth category of spirit, the Holy Spirit which is *". . . the mediator of the light of holiness, . . ."*[17] man would be only as he was, let us say, when formed of dust, before God had breathed into him the breath of life; for the spirit of faith is brought to mankind by the Prophets of God; *". . . it invests the world of humanity with a new life and endows human realities with a new spirit."* [18]

To show what man is, 'Abdu'l-Bahá often contrasts him with the animal, with that phenomenon which manifests spirit only in the first and second degrees:

> Verily God has created the animal in the image and likeness of man, for though man outwardly is human, yet in nature he possesses animal tendencies.[19]

> Man is like the animal in physical structure but otherwise immeasurably separated and superior.[20]

He does not disdain animals, He loves them, for Bahá'-u'lláh has established not only the rights of man, but the rights of animals as well. He says that man can learn from animals, and describes such animal behavior as man could emulate:

> Among the animals racial prejudice does not exist. Consider the doves; there is no distinction as to whether it is an oriental or an occidental dove.[21]

Throughout the kingdoms of living organisms there is sex differentiation in function, but no preference or distinction is made in favour of either male or female. In the animal kingdom individual sex exists, but rights are equal and without distinction.[22]

He points out that in some ways the animal is superior to man: *". . . the animal is often superior to man in sense perception."*[23] It is simply that 'Abdu'l-Bahá does not wish man to be an animal; that he who is free should enslave himself in the five senses, renouncing his own peculiar powers—like a bird walking or an orator making meaningless sounds.

'Abdu'l-Bahá says that *"Manifestly the animal has been created for the life of this world."*[24] Animals can easily be happy here, not man:

Consider how difficult for man is the attainment of pleasures and happiness in this mortal world. How easy it is for the animal. . . . The animal is nobler, more serene and confident, because each hour is free from anxiety . . . but man, restless and dissatisfied, runs from morn till eve. . . . His life is intended to be a life of spiritual enjoyment to which the animal can never attain.[25]

Never, perhaps, has material civilization reached a higher point and been more widespread than in the United States today, and yet Americans are spending annually billions of dollars for alcohol, psychiatrists, and happiness pills to enable them to bear it.

The Master said:

In cities like New York the people are submerged in the sea of materialism. Their sensibilities are attuned to material forces, their perceptions purely physical. The animal energies predominate in their activities; all their thoughts are directed to material things; day and night they are devoted to the attractions of this world, without aspiration beyond the life that is vanishing and mortal. In schools and temples of learning[,] knowledge of the sciences acquired is based upon material observations only; there is no realization of divinity in their methods and conclusions—all have reference to the world of matter. They are not interested in attaining knowledge of the mysteries of God or understanding the secrets of the heavenly kingdom; what they acquire is based altogether upon visible and tangible evidences . . . they . . . are utterly out of touch with God. . . .[26]

He often laughingly said that the donkey and cow were far superior to the materialistic philosophers of the day:

All the animals are materialists. . . . They have no knowledge of the divine Prophets and Holy

Books—mere captives of nature and the sense world. In reality they are like the great philosophers of this day who are not in touch with God and the Holy Spirit—deniers of the Prophets, ignorant of spiritual susceptibilities, deprived of the heavenly bounties and without belief in the supernatural power. The animal lives this kind of life blissfully and untroubled, whereas the material philosophers labor and study for ten or twenty years in schools and colleges, denying God, the Holy Spirit and divine inspirations. The animal is even a greater philosopher, for it attains the ability to do this without labor and study. For instance, the cow denies God and the Holy Spirit, knows nothing of divine inspirations, heavenly bounties or spiritual emotions and is a stranger to the world of hearts. Like the philosophers, the cow is a captive of nature and knows nothing beyond the range of the senses. The philosophers, however, glory in this, saying, "We are not captives of superstitions; we have implicit faith in the impressions of the senses and know nothing beyond the realm of nature, which contains and covers everything." But the cow, without study or proficiency in the sciences, modestly and quietly views life from the same standpoint. . . .

This is not the glory of man. The glory of man is in the knowledge of God, spiritual susceptibilities, attainment to transcendent powers and the bounties of the Holy Spirit. . . . Is the intellect of these people greater than the intellect of Christ? . . . He attached little importance to this material life, denying Himself rest and composure, accepting trials and voluntarily suffering vicissitudes because He was endowed with spiritual susceptibilities and the power of the Holy Spirit.[27]

The Qur'án says:

Thou gavest them and their fathers their fill of good things, till they forget the remembrance of Thee, and became a lost people.[28]

And again:

And be ye not like those who forget God, and whom He hath therefore caused to forget their own selves.[29]

The Master teaches that only the Manifestations of God, the focal centers of the Holy Spirit, can recall man to himself:

The holy Manifestations of God come into the world to dispel the darkness of the animal, or physical, nature of man, to purify him from his imperfections in order that his heavenly and spiritual nature may become quickened, his divine qualities awakened . . . and [that] all the virtues of the world of humanity latent within him may come to life. These holy Manifestations of God are the Educators and Trainers of the world of existence, the Teachers. . . . Men are ignorant; the Manifestations of God make them wise. They are animalistic; the Manifestations make them human. They are savage and cruel; the Manifestations lead them into kingdoms of light and love. They are unjust; the Manifestations cause them to become just. Man is selfish; They sever him from self and desire. Man is haughty; They make him meek, humble and friendly. He is earthly; They make him heavenly. Men are material; the Manifestations transform them into divine semblance. They are immature children; the Manifestations develop them into maturity. Man is poor; They endow him with wealth. Man is base, treacherous and mean; the Manifestations of God uplift him into dignity, nobility and loftiness.[30]

"Man," further says 'Abdu'l-Bahá, *"is a reality which stands between light and darkness."*[31] He has a material body and a *"heavenly body"*[32] or inner reality:

So to speak, the reality of man is clad in the outer garment of the animal, the habiliments of the world

35

of nature, the world of darkness, imperfections and unlimited baseness. On the other hand, we find in him justice, sincerity, faithfulness, knowledge, wisdom, illumination, mercy and pity, coupled with intellect, comprehension, the power to grasp the realities of things. . . .[33]

Man attains to all good things through his "second birth," that is, through the orientation of his soul toward the Manifestation of God, and *"[w]ere it not for the coming of these holy Manifestations of God, all mankind would be found on the plane of the animal."*[34]

To conclude these few allusions to 'Abdu'l-Bahá's infinite teachings on man, there is this:

The station of man is great, very great. God has created man after His own image and likeness. He has endowed him with a mighty power which is capable of discovering the mysteries of phenomena. . . . As he possesses sense endowment in common with the animals, it is evident that he is distinguished above them by his conscious power of penetrating abstract realities. He acquires divine wisdom; he searches out the mysteries of creation; he witnesses the radiance of omnipotence; he attains the second birth—that is to say, he is born out of the material world just as he is born of the mother; he attains to everlasting life;

he draws nearer to God; his heart is replete with the love of God. This is the foundation of the world of humanity; this is the image and likeness of God; this is the reality of man; otherwise he is an animal.[35]

And lastly,

Thus, the divinity of God, which is the totality of all perfections, reveals itself in the reality of man. . . . If man did not exist, the universe would be without result, for the purpose of existence is the revelation of the divine perfections.[36]

How to Kill Prejudice

In spite of His own immaculate perfection, the Master never turned away from the despised and the rejected, but rather transformed them with His regal touch. Florence <u>Kh</u>ánum tells in her book of her reaction to some of the people she saw in her travels. (It must be remembered that she was Boston-educated, which means that she took a rather conservative view of the rest of mankind). She writes of a little servant:

> I . . . discovered to my amazement and shock, that the expression of her eyes was more wild and uncivilized than the eyes of our domestic animals in America! Such as the eyes of our horses, our dogs, our cats, which usually give back a reflection of our love and affection, while this young girl's eyes did not!

She grew somewhat afraid of the local people, and then one day she saw a native woman coming along the roofed-over stone corridor, and she wanted to run away. Just then 'Abdu'l-Bahá approached with one of His daughters:

> I saw the woman pause, bow, and greet the Master. He replied graciously, and spoke sweetly, and as He passed, pressed a coin into her hand. She burst forth into phrases of evident joy and gratitude, and went away. I lingered, to ask the Master's daughter: "What did she say? Who is she?"
>
> "She is the daughter of a desert chief, and she has suffered very much."
>
> "Is she a Bahá'í?"
>
> "No; but she loves the Master very much. He has been kind to her."
>
> "What did she say to Him?"
>
> "She said she would pray for Him."
>
> "And what did the Master say?"
>
> "He thanked her."
>
> In my American-trained mind, at first I thought: "How presumptuous for that dirty-looking, half-savage-looking woman to tell the Master she would pray for Him!" And then, as the sweetness and humility of His reply astonished me, another experience of His spiritual grandeur overwhelmed my soul.

'Abdu'l-Bahá was to say:

> . . . there is need of a superior power to overcome human prejudices; a power which nothing in the world of mankind can withstand and which will overshadow the effect of all other forces at work in human conditions. That irresistible power is the love of God.[1]

Man, the Preoccupied

We would feel worse about the hideous news, typical of reports from many countries, which show how the social fabric is now rotting away, if we and our fellow-believers had not spent almost our entire lives trying to tell of the advent of the Manifestation; if five generations of Bahá'ís had not done so; if the Báb's young body had not been smashed by seven hundred Persian bullets; if, to diffuse this message, 20,000 martyrs had not died; if Bahá'u'lláh had not spent His entire adulthood and age as a Prisoner, chained, bastinadoed, banished; if 'Abdu'l-Bahá had not sacrificed every ounce of His strength, His whole life long, to this Cause; if the Guardian had not given to it all the days of his life.

We have tried, each in his degree, and the best way we knew, to deliver this message for the regeneration of mankind. And every day we have heard from the world (when it did not attack us and drive us out) the same preoccupied, polite response:

> I must go to my church (or mosque, or synagogue)—I have my own private religion: to do good—Sorry, no time now—Religion is superstition—I know better than Jesus—No one can be saved except in my religion—Foreigners are no good—Why are there so few of you?—You can't change human nature—Your teachings are too good to be true.

"For a whole century," the Guardian writes, "God has respited mankind, that it might acknowledge the Founder of such a Revelation, espouse His Cause, proclaim His greatness, and establish His Order."[1]

In the same work, *The Promised Day is Come*, Shoghi Effendi quotes Bahá'u'lláh's dire prophecy: *"The time for the destruction of the world and its people hath arrived. The hour is approaching when the most great convulsion will have appeared."*[2]

"After Doom, what?" asked an American friend. After God has inflicted His great wound, He will heal it, and then the restoring presence of the Master's spirit will be felt around the world.

The Development of Love

"Let not a man glory in this, that he can kill his fellow crea-
tures;" says the Master, *"nay, rather, let him glory in this,*
that he can love them."[1] His life was one long expression of
love. In America He said:

> I have come here to visit you. With the greatest
> longing I have wished to see you. Realizing it was
> only with great difficulty that you could come to me
> and that very few could make the trip, I decided to
> come to you. . . . Praise be to God! I am here, and
> I am looking into your faces—faces radiant with
> inner beauty, hearts attracted to the Kingdom of
> Abhá, spirits exhilarated through the glad tidings
> of God. Therefore, I have experienced the greatest
> possible happiness. And surely this happiness must
> be mutual, for the hearts are connected with each

other and are filled with the same vibration. . . . If we should offer a hundred thousand thanksgivings every moment to the threshold of God for this love which has blended the Orient and Occident, we would fail to express our gratitude sufficiently. If all the powers of earth should seek to bring about this love between East and West, they would prove incapable. If they wished to establish this unity, it would prove impossible. But Bahá'u'lláh has accomplished both . . . and this bond of unity through love is indissoluble. It shall continue unto time everlasting, and day by day its power shall increase. Erelong it shall enchain the world, and eventually the hearts of all the nations of the world will be brought together by its constraining clasp.[2]

And later, at a Feast:

Behold how the power of Bahá'u'lláh has brought the East and West together. And 'Abdu'l-Bahá is standing, serving you. There is neither rod nor blow, whip nor sword; but the power of the love of God has accomplished this.[3]

Reading His introductory remarks to audiences, one has the feeling that day after day He was addressing a superior order of being; and yet they were just people, transformed by His own love:

Although I am weary after my long journey, the light of the spirit shining in your faces brings me rest and reward.[4]

Tonight I am very happy for I have come here to meet my friends. I consider you my relatives, my companions. . . .[5]

. . . I ask you to accept 'Abdu'l-Bahá as your servant.[6]

This to the poor in New York's Bowery: *"Today I have been speaking from dawn until now, yet because of love, fellowship and desire to be with you, I have come here to speak again. . . ."*[7] A meeting where Negro and white were present was *"a beautiful bouquet of violets gathered together in varying colours, dark and light."*[8] To a children's meeting: *"You are all my children, my spiritual children. Spiritual children are dearer than physical children, for it is possible for physical children to turn away from the spirit of God. . . ."*[9]

Praise be to God! It is with a deep realization of happiness that I am present here this evening, for I am looking upon the faces of those who are earnest in their search for reality and who sincerely long to attain knowledge of truth.[10]

One cannot help contrasting the way a current Protestant evangelist addresses his audiences: "God looks at you . . .

with His magnifying glass and sees your faults. . . . You are guilty! You are guilty! You are guilty!"[11] Or Martin Luther, as quoted by R. H. Bainton in *Here I Stand*:

> I understand that this is the week for the church collection and many of you do not want to give a thing. You ungrateful people should be ashamed of yourselves . . . now that you are asked to give four miserable pennies you are up in arms. . . . I am not saying this for myself. I receive nothing from you. I am the prince's beggar. But I am sorry I ever freed you from the tyrants and the papists. You ungrateful beasts, you are not worthy of the treasure of the gospel. If you don't improve, I will stop preaching rather than cast pearls before swine.

'Abdu'l-Bahá's love has not left the world simply because He is now hidden from our eyes. Florence Khánum has this to say, of a long-ago moment when she was in His presence, and was thinking of those deprived of it not by time but by the curve of the planet: for no believer living in those days could think of the world without 'Abdu'l-Bahá:

> One noon, my heart overflowing with happiness and gratitude for the great good fortune of such an experience in the Holy household, I ventured to remark

to 'Abdu'l-Bahá: "I wish all the Bahá'ís in America could attain to 'Akká." (In those days the expression for a visit to 'Akká was this: attaining to 'Akká). 'Abdu'l-Bahá paused a moment before answering and then replied, *"I am ever with those who love me."*

Love is Not Enough

He teaches, however, that society must be founded on justice, not love or forgiveness. Bahá'u'lláh has named our central administrative institutions Houses of Justice, and these bodies, called at present Spiritual Assemblies, relate particularly to the Master; perhaps one reason for this is that they are the most effective agency for the changing of human nature, and man's perfectibility is always the Master's *leit motif.* Of them He has written:

> These Spiritual Assemblies are aided by the Spirit of God. Their defender is 'Abdu'l-Bahá. Over them He spreadeth His wings.[1]

From the Bahá'ís, functioning in these Assemblies according to methods taught by the Master, the whole world will learn how to discover, through unity, prayer and consultation, what is justice in any given situation, and how to apply it. *"In this Cause,"* He said, *"consultation is of vital importance, but spiritual conference and not the mere voicing of personal views is intended."*[2]

Then He tells of a visit which He made to the Legislature of a Western power:

> . . . the experience was not impressive. Parliamentary procedure should have for its object the attainment of the light of truth upon questions presented and not furnish a battle ground for opposition and self-opinion. Antagonism and contradiction are unfortunate and always destructive to truth. In the parliamentary meeting mentioned, altercation and useless quibbling were frequent; . . . even in one instance a physical encounter took place between two members. It was not consultation but comedy.[3]

He has never, notwithstanding this statement, taught that people during consultation must agree with one another; on the contrary, He says, *"The shining spark of truth cometh forth only after the clash of differing opinions."*[4] The word only is important in this context. Agreement takes place following consultation, and the decision will preferably be unanimous, but in any case the voice of the majority must be wholeheartedly accepted. The Master always stands for order, not anarchy. He says:

The essence of the Bahá'í spirit is that, in order to establish a better social order and economic condition, there must be allegiance to the laws and principles of government.[5]

Criminals, He says, must not go unpunished; society must be protected from them; personal vengeance is forbidden to Bahá'ís, but *". . . the body politic has the right to preserve and to protect. It holds no grudge and harbours no enmity . . ."*[6] for the given criminal. He says that if unresisted, Attila *"would not have left a single soul alive"*[7] and that *"the proper functioning of the body politic depends upon justice and not forgiveness."*[8] In explaining Christ's words about turning the other cheek (Luke 6:29) He says *"it was for the purpose of teaching men not to take personal revenge,"*[9] and continued,

So what Christ meant by forgiveness and magnanimity is not that if another nation were to assail you; burn your homes; plunder your possessions; assault your wives, children, and kin; and violate your honour, you must submit to that tyrannical host and permit them to carry out every manner of iniquity and oppression. Rather, the words of Christ refer to private transactions between two individuals, stating that if one person assaults another, the injured party should forgive. But the body politic must safeguard the rights of man. Thus, if someone were to attack, injure, oppress, and wound me, I would in no wise oppose him but would show forgiveness. But if someone were to attack Siyyid Manshádí here, I would of course prevent him.[10]

We read that when, in 1922, 5,000 Mennonites went down to Mexico from Canada in order to continue living according to their own interpretation of the Bible, and had purchased for their colony 200,000 acres from a vast ranch in Chihuahua, a revolutionary named Pancho Villa held sway there, "and the surrounding hills swarmed with his fierce Villistas, who learned soon that the Mennonite men would not raise their fists in anger. Time after time the Villistas forayed down from the hills to rape the blonde Mennonite women while their men stood by and prayed in helpless anguish."[11]

Florence Khánum was taught by the early believers that each action of the Master's, each word, "has not only a literal meaning but in it are wrapped up untold spiritual, future meanings." He lived not only in the moment but for all time. "His acts, His words, are as when one throws a stone into the water, and the rings of water continue on and on. . . . So do the Master's deeds and words eternally reveal their inner bounties throughout the life here, and hereafter!" One day, she relates, "before we rose from the table, I saw the Master look at some object on the floor. I followed His gaze, and saw a strange black insect swiftly approaching my chair. The Master arose, and putting His foot down firmly on it, killed the creature. *'This kind,'* He said, as He resumed His chair, *'is poisonous.'"*

The Trap of Imitation

The great weapon of every vested interest on earth is man's faculty of mindless imitation of his forebears. What he is taught in his early years operates throughout his life in the same way as post-hypnotic suggestion; many an action of his, many an opinion, was put into his mind beforehand, and as he carries it out, he offers an apparently rational explanation of his behavior. Certain religionists say, "Give us the child in his first five years and we will keep him always." This blind imitation is 'Abdu'l-Bahá's main target; He spearheads His attack against it; after all, the Faith He teaches can bear adult investigation.

"Verily mind is the supreme gift of God,"[1] the Master says, and again, ". . . *the precious, priceless bestowal of God—the human mind. . . .*"[2] He tells us:

The human spirit, which distinguishes man from the animal, is the rational soul, and these two terms—

the human spirit and the rational soul—designate one and the same thing. . . . As for the mind, it is the power of the human spirit. . . . Spirit is as the tree, and the mind as the fruit.[3]

How can man believe that which he knows to be opposed to reason? Is this possible? Can the heart accept that which reason denies? Reason is the first faculty of man, and the religion of God is in harmony with it.[4]

Because of blind imitation, the Jews crucified Jesus:

Notwithstanding the fulfilment of all the prophetic signs in Christ, the Jews denied Him and entered the period of their deprivation because of their allegiance to imitations and ancestral forms.

. . . In reality His Holiness Christ proclaimed and completed the law of Moses. He was the very helper and assister of Moses. He spread the Book of Moses throughout the world. . . . The Jews did not comprehend this, and the cause of their ignorance was blind and tenacious adherence to imitations of ancient forms and teachings; therefore they finally sentenced Christ to death.[5]

"[T]he people of religion," 'Abdu'l-Bahá teaches,

are of two kinds: Some worship the sun, and some adore the dawning points from which the sun rises. . . . When that Sun of Reality with its divine bestowal, its heavenly glow and effulgence transferred to the Messianic point of rising, the Jews denied its appearance in Jesus, for they were not worshipers of the Sun itself but adored its rising in Moses. . . .

What was the reason of this deprivation? It was simply because they were imitating fathers and ancestors in forms of belief instead of turning towards the Sun of Divinity.[6]

He refutes such Christian beliefs as original sin on the grounds of their being unreasonable:

Even if we should see a governor, an earthly ruler punishing a son for the wrong-doing of his father, we would look upon that ruler as an unjust man. . . . If the father of a thousand generations [back] committed a sin, is it just to demand that the present generation should suffer the consequences thereof?[7]

The Catholic Church teaches that since Adam's Fall, the soul is born deprived of sanctifying grace, in a state of sin, which has to be remitted by baptism; for this reason, when labor proves difficult, a priest will baptize the infant *in utero* (see Philip Wylie, *Generation of Vipers*), since unbaptized children are, the Church teaches, excluded from heaven; in the case of a head presentation, baptism is administered on the head, otherwise on the part presented. (For such details the writer has consulted authorized Catholic sources as found in all well-equipped public libraries).

The Master says of children who die, after or before the appointed time of birth:

> These children abide under the shadow of the Divine Providence, and, as they have committed no sin and are unsullied by the defilements of the world of nature, they will become the manifestations of divine bounty and the glances of the eye of divine mercy will be directed towards them.[8]

Satan, who plays such an important role in various religions, does not exist, the Master says:

> . . . Satan or whatever is interpreted as evil, refers to the lower nature in man. . . . God has never created an evil spirit; all such ideas and nomenclature are symbols expressing the mere human or earthly nature of man. It is an essential condition of the soil of earth that thorns, weeds and fruitless trees may grow from it. Relatively speaking, this is evil; it is simply the lower state and baser product of nature.[9]

In explaining one meaning of the Adam and Eve story—and the Master says there are many—He tells us that *"by 'Adam' is meant the spirit of Adam and by 'Eve' is meant His self"*;* the tree is this world, and the serpent is *"attachment to the material world."*[10] *"For when the spirit and the self of Adam became attached to the material world, they passed from the realm of freedom into the realm of bondage; this condition was perpetuated with each succeeding generation, and this attachment of spirit and self to the material world—which is sin—was inherited by His descendants."*[11] Jesus died *"to ensure the remission of sins—that is, the detachment of spirits from the material world and their attraction to the divine realm. . . ."*[12]

The Master does not mean that we should abandon our daily life and the business of living; He says only that *". . . the energies of the heart must not be attached to these things; the soul must not be completely occupied with them."*[13]

Explaining Jesus' statement *"I am the bread which came down from heaven,"* the Master says:

It was not the body of Christ which came from heaven. His body came from the womb of Mary. . . . The Spirit of Christ and not the body descended

---

* A closer translation of the original (nafs) as used here would be "self."

from heaven. The body of Christ was but human. . . . Consequently, by saying He was the bread which came from heaven He meant that the perfections which He showed forth were divine perfections . . . He said, "If any man eat of this bread, he shall live for ever." That is to say, whosoever assimilates these divine perfections which are within me will never die; whosoever has a share and partakes of these heavenly bounties I embody will find eternal life. . . .[14]

Unless people investigating the Bahá'í Faith will oblige themselves to become as neutral as a scientist making a laboratory test; unless they will look at their own selves, their heredity and their environment (for three factors are involved, the Master says, not two—since the soul has individuality, personality),[15] and deliberately assess these influences on their judgement, 'Abdu'l-Bahá's words on blind imitation can never be meaningful to them. To form mechanical words and gestures and thoughts, to keep on going through the motions, to hold uninvestigated opinions, is to be what the Prophets of God call dead.

He calls the Prophets *"the first teachers," "universal educators,"*[16] and continues:

Forms and imitations which creep in afterward . . . are clouds which obscure the Sun of Reality. If you reflect upon the essential teachings of Jesus, you will realize that they are the light of the world. Nobody can question their truth. . . . The forms and superstitions which appeared and obscured the light did not affect the reality of Christ. . . . Jesus Christ said, "Put up thy sword into the sheath." The meaning is that warfare is forbidden and abrogated; but consider the Christian wars which took place afterward. Christian hostility and inquisition spared not even the learned; he who proclaimed the revolution of the earth was imprisoned; he who announced the new astronomical system was persecuted as a heretic; scholars and scientists became objects of fanatical hatred, and many were killed and tortured. How do these actions conform with the teachings of Jesus Christ, and what relation do they bear to His own example? . . . How can hatred, hostility and persecution be reconciled with Christ and His teachings?[17]

He wished every religionist to study the basic teachings of the Prophets:

The fundamental principles of the Prophets are correct and true. The imitations and superstitions which have crept in are at wide variance with the original precepts and commands.[18]

This study will unify all religions, since *"the religions are essentially one and the same."*[19] It is only the second division of religion the *"social laws and regulations"*[20] which change from one dispensation to another; the food laws have changed; the marriage laws; the law regarding interest on money; the Sabbath, and many more; in the law of Moses, if a man stole his hand was cut off; if a man cursed his father, he was put to death (Exodus 21:17); if a man broke the law of the Sabbath he was put to death (Exodus 35:2); such laws are for their time, not for all time; the following dispensation changes or retains them, according to the world's needs as determined by the Manifestation of God.[21]

The Bahá'í Faith is the first in history to insist on the independent investigation of truth; 'Abdu'l-Bahá teaches that " *[m]an is not intended to see through the eyes of another, hear through another's ears nor comprehend with another's brain."*[22] Man *"must not be an imitator or blind follower of any soul. He must not rely implicitly upon the opinion of any man without investigation; nay, each soul must seek intelligently and independently. . . ."*[23] Ignorance based upon blind imitation causes wars, hatreds, untold suffering. This does not mean that having found truth in any given direction a man should keep on seeking it; his act of seeking it would prove that he had not found it. For example, 'Abdu'l-Bahá says that *". . . the outward is the expression of the inward: The earthly realm is the mirror of the heavenly Kingdom, and the material world is in accordance with the spiritual world,* "[24] and that the sun is the symbol of the Manifestation of God:

> This Sun of Reality, this Centre of effulgences, is the Prophet or Manifestation of God. Just as the phenomenal sun shines upon the material world producing life and growth, likewise, the spiritual or prophetic Sun confers illumination upon the human world of thought and intelligence, and unless it rose upon the horizon of human existence, the kingdom of man would become dark and extinguished.[25]

Now, if a soul becomes convinced through his own investigations that Bahá'u'lláh is the Manifestation of God for our day, he should believe the teachings of Bahá'u'lláh and not go looking for another Manifestation before *"the expiration of a full thousand years."* [26] He should believe the *"central authoritative Personage"* [27] appointed by Bahá'u'lláh to protect His Faith from schism, and obey him in the way a man, volunteering for the army, obeys an authorized superior officer. If some people do not understand the hidden secret of one of His commands and actions, they ought not to oppose it, for the universal Manifestation does what He wishes.[28] It is only reasonable that if a soul believes these teachings, he should obey them; before believing in them, he is asked to investigate them to his heart's content.

Christians are disturbed when they read in the Bahá'í writings that Muḥammad is a true Prophet of God. The Jews were deeply troubled when, in the United States, the Master told them to acknowledge Jesus Christ; any effort to go against the current of imitation is painful. Among the things He said to them were these: Christ did not invalidate the Torah, He spread it; Christians and Muslims accept Moses;

What harm could result to the Jewish people, then, if they in return should accept Christ and acknowledge the validity of the Prophethood of Muḥammad?[29]

To the Jews at Temple Emmanuel in San Francisco:

Why do you not say that Christ was the Word of God? Why do you not speak these few words that will do away with all this difficulty? Then there will be no more hatred and fanaticism, no more warfare and bloodshed in the Land of Promise.[30]

He then solemnly declared His own belief in Moses as a most noteworthy Prophet and Revealer of the Law of God, a Founder of civilization, and asked, *"Have I lost anything by saying this to you and believing it as a Bahá'í? On the contrary, it benefits me. . . ."*[31] Every nation is proud of its great men; *"What harm, then, could come from your declaration that Jesus of Nazareth was a great man of Israelitish birth and, therefore, we love Him?"* [32] And He warned, *"The time may come when in Europe itself they will arise against the Jews."* [33] The Master Himself describes some of the reaction to His addresses to the Jews: *"The address delivered last evening in the Jewish synagogue* [Washington] *evidently disturbed some of the people, including the revered rabbi who called upon me this afternoon. Together we went over the ground again. . . ."* [34] He tells how, at the end of their meeting, the rabbi said, "'I believe that what you have said is perfectly true, but I must ask one thing of you. Will you not tell the Christians to love us a little more?'"[35] The Master replied, *"We have advised them and will continue to do so."* [36] The year was 1912; some twenty years more, and the Jewish people were to see the massacre, in Europe, of an estimated five million souls, perhaps one third of their race.

Mankind is
One People

The New Testament says that God *"hath made of one blood all nations of men for to dwell on all the face of the earth,"*[1] but it is obvious that Christians do not believe this. If they did, they would not practice racial segregation, crowd the people of this or that race into separate parts of town or else banish them entirely, tell them they are under a curse, or repudiate social intercourse and intermarriage with them. This cruel and indeed suicidal behavior, perpetuated by imitation, is based on just one factor: ignorance. For the oneness of mankind, the pivotal principle of Bahá'u'lláh, is not a counsel of perfection but a laboratory fact; one does not have to beg anybody to believe it.

'Abdu'l-Bahá teaches of the atom's journeyings throughout creation. He says the elemental atoms are in *"the progressive and perpetual motion . . . throughout the various degrees of phenomena and the kingdoms of existence."*[2] He traces the atoms' journeyings from mineral to vegetable to animal to man, and back to mineral again, each atom sequentially *"imbued with the powers and virtues of the kingdoms it traverses . . . also reflects the attributes and qualities of the forms and organisms of those kingdoms."* [3] *". . . All things are involved in all things,"* the Master quotes from the Arabian philosophers. *"It is evident that each material organism is an aggregate expression of single and simple elements, and a given cellular element or atom has its coursings or journeyings through . . . myriad stages of life."* [4] At death, the elements which composed the body are dispersed, and although reincarnation cannot take place since no identity occurs more than once in the world (in all the world's granaries no two grains of wheat are alike). *"The sign of Divine Unity is present and visible in all things."* [5] It can come about *"that certain constituents of the former body entered into the composition of the latter. . . ."* [6] One asks oneself how the racist is going to stop this perpetual journeying of the atoms, and how he is going to shut the atoms out.

Show Forth
True Economics

Of the Bahá'í Temple the Master teaches, *"Its gates will be flung wide open to mankind. . . ."* [1] This is how His own door was. People always crowded around Him, unable to stay away. He said,

> The supreme need of humanity is co-operation and reciprocity. . . . A tree can live solitary and alone, but this is impossible for man without retrogression. Therefore, every co-operative attitude and activity of human life is praiseworthy. . . . [2]

At the time of Florence <u>Kh</u>ánum's pilgrimage in 1906, He was still a prisoner. She saw with indignation the heavy bars at the window, the sentry pacing outside; and she watched, gratified and exultant, 'Abdu'l-Bahá's kingly reception of a steady stream of people of all ranks, from notables to the desperately poor—those poor who always had first claim on Him and who, as He told them in the Bowery, were His friends and family, and resembled Jesus more than the rich.[3] His extensive teachings on economics are summed up in these words:

> Manifest true economics to the people. Show what love is, what kindness is, what true severance is and generosity. . . . Act in accordance with the teachings of Bahá'u'lláh. All His Books will be translated. . . . Let your deeds be the real translation of their meaning.[4]

He has entrusted the have-nots to the haves; in future the rich will *"most willingly extend assistance to the poor and take steps to establish these economic adjustments permanently,"*[5] unable to rest while they know of anyone in want. Eleanor Roosevelt has described how, as the President's wife, she could not induce her powerful friends to get out of their automobiles and accompany her into the slum-dwellings of the poor. Bahá'u'lláh writes:

> If ye meet the abased or the downtrodden, turn not away disdainfully from them, for the King of Glory ever watcheth over them and surroundeth them with such tenderness as none can fathom. . . . O ye rich ones of the earth! Flee not from the face of the poor that lieth in the dust, nay rather befriend him

and suffer him to recount the tale of the woes with which God's inscrutable Decree hath caused him to be afflicted. By the righteousness of God! Whilst ye consort with him, the Concourse on high will be looking upon you, will be interceding for you, will be extolling your names and glorifying your action.[6]

The Master teaches that the rich must go and look at poverty face-to-face; and this was His way, all the days of His life.

The Assassin's Prisoner

'Abdu'l-Bahá was the prisoner of 'Abdu'l-Ḥamíd. This Sultan, a man pale under his rouge, emaciated, hollow-cheeked, hooked-nosed, with a badly-dyed reddish-brown beard, rickety legs, a thin hand mechanically caressing the heavy, dyed moustache that hid the mouth with its cruel, thin, upper lip, its sensual lower one—with a bulging forehead under his enormous red fez, and heavy-lidded eyes now vacant, now angry or terrified, had schemed his way to the throne.[1]

> He is a skilful layer of traps, and capable of all kinds of abjectness toward his enemies when he fears them and of the greatest cruelty when he has them in his power, and he enjoys his vengeance all the more for having patiently nourished it in secret.
>
> Not only is the life of a man who is troublesome to him nothing to him, but spilled blood seems

to calm and soothe his shattered nerves, always stretched to the snapping point. "At night, before going to sleep," says one of his chamberlains, "he has someone read to him. His favourite books are those giving detailed accounts of assassinations and executions. The stories of crimes excite him and prevent him from sleeping, but as soon as his reader reaches a passage where blood flows, the Sultan immediately becomes calm and falls asleep."[2]

'Abdu'l-Ḥamíd could never get warm, even though he reportedly wore a suit of mail under his clothes. He washed himself every few minutes at washstands placed in every corner. In his kitchen, a small barred cell like a "huge safe," his chef worked always under the eye of a court official; when ready, the dishes were brought to him covered with a black cloth, its ends sealed with this official's seal; even so, the Sultan would often make the official taste the food first, or would try it out on a cat or dog. His main pursuit in life was reading the reports of his spies—papers that had to be passed through a disinfecting oven before he would touch them. His main dread (an apt one: Gladstone called him "The Great Assassin") was of being murdered.[3] His clothes were a web of secret pockets to hold his spies' reports, and his three revolvers. Above all, he feared any sudden gesture in his direction, or rapid step. When such happened, he had been known to shoot and kill.

It was this man who had 'Abdu'l-Bahá's life in his cold hands. It was to him that, as the Master records in His Will and Testament, the breakers of Bahá'u'lláh's Covenant, under the Arch-Breaker, the Master's half-brother, sent in their calumnies: that He had hoisted the flag of revolt, built a fortress and vast ammunition depot on Mount Carmel, raised an army of 30,000 men, and conspired with English and American supporters, who were flocking to Him in large numbers and in disguise, to take over the surrounding provinces and ultimately to usurp the power of the Sultan himself.[4]

Five years before Florence Khánum's pilgrimage, 'Abdu'l-Hamíd had stringently reimposed the Master's imprisonment, whose restrictions had been gradually relaxed. Secret agents traveled back and forth between 'Akká and Constantinople, and spies watched everywhere, while 'Abdu'l-Bahá, "alone and unaided," was subjected to prolonged interrogation by judges and officials. He refuted every one of the charges, as absurd as they were infamous, and expressed to the court His ardent wish to be put to death for the Faith, so that He could share the sufferings of the beloved Báb.[5]

A year following her pilgrimage, another, notorious Commission sailed into 'Akká by order of the Sultan, took over the Telegraph and Postal services, dismissed officials considered friendly to 'Abdu'l-Bahá, and established themselves in the city. The Covenant-breakers were jubilant; the townspeople stood by to watch when the Master should be carried away on the ship, and at this time even some of the poor forsook Him.[6] Then the Commission sailed down to Haifa to inspect the Báb's sepulcher, which 'Abdu'l-Bahá was constructing on Mount Carmel, and one day about sunset the ship was seen heading up the coast again toward 'Akká. As His family and the believers wept, the Master walked, alone in the dusk, up and down, up and down in the courtyard of His house. Suddenly the lights of the ship swung round, and she changed her course and sailed away in the direction of Constantinople.

Later on when the Commission's report was submitted to 'Abdu'l-Ḥamíd, it aroused little response: a bomb had just been exploded in his path, on his way home from his Friday prayers at the mosque. In 1908, the following year, the "Young Turk" Revolution closed the case forever. Of His royal jailer, the Master says only this:

[Bahá'u'lláh] *was under the dominion of 'Abdu'l-Ḥamíd. I, too, was in the prison of 'Abdu'l-Ḥamíd until the Committee of Union and Progress hoisted the standard of liberty and my fetters were removed.*"[7]

They lifted the chains from my neck and threw them around the neck of Abdu'l-Ḥamíd. That which he did to me was inflicted upon him. Now the position is precisely reversed. His days are spent in prison just as I passed the days in prison at 'Akká, with this difference: that I was happy in imprisonment. . . . I was not a criminal. They had imprisoned me in the path of God. . . . I was happy that . . . I was a prisoner in the Cause of God, that my life was not wasted. . . . Nobody who saw me imagined that I was in prison.[8]

'Abdu'l-Bahá's Birthday

Florence Khánum was in 'Abdu'l-Bahá's presence on two of His birthdays, in 1906 and 1912. On the latter occasion He spoke at the Cambridge* home of her parents, Mr. and Mrs. Francis W. Breed.[1] Writing of the 1906 birthday she says:

> Remembering birthday festivities in America, and how the one for whom festivities were given, though host or hostess, was the central figure, and guest of honor, I queried, "How will 'Abdu'l-Bahá act on His birthday? Will He, for once, lie in bed, late in the morning, while His family and the house guests file by to . . . offer any gift, and to wish Him the happy returns of the day? . . . Won't it seem strange to see 'Abdu'l-Bahá graciously accepting our homage? The

---

* Massachusetts.

great Exemplar of Servitude . . . being served?" I could not envisage the picture; yet I hoped that the One Who always served from earliest morning to late at night would rest and enjoy leisure and let His loving friends and followers offer Him their feeble services.

I saw a group of eight lambs or so, newly arrived in the courtyard, and was told they would be sacrificed for the Feast of the morrow, and that quite a large company of men and women Bahá'ís would assemble for the celebration. The following morning I awoke late. . . . For once I had not been called as usual, to the early morning prayers. . . . Soon after, Khán appeared, and said, "Since early dawn, the Master has been busy. . . . Over two hundred guests are expected for the Feast, and the Master has been at work, since dawn." I exclaimed, "The Master working on His birthday?" "Oh! You should have seen Him! . . . They tell me He has been kneading, with His own hands, dough for the ovens. He has been in gay spirits, inspiring, uplifting, cheering all His helpers." The picture I had envisioned, of 'Abdu'l-Bahá reclining . . . all the morning, while we paid Him homage, vanished in my astonishment! Later, Khán returned radiant and enthusiastic to our room. He said that 'Abdu'l-Bahá assisted in passing the platters . . . the rice . . . the lamb . . . the fruits of the region (of such large size, such color, and such fragrance as only the sunshine of the East produces and paints). Moving among His two hundred guests, He spoke to them as He served them, such Divine words of love and spiritual import. Khán particularly recalled His words to this effect: "*If one of you has been wounded in heart by the words or deeds of another, during the past year, forgive him now; that in purity of heart and loving pardon, you may feast in happiness, and arise, renewed in spirit.*"

For 'Abdu'l-Bahá teaches that in whatever mood we sit down to eat, that mood is actually strengthened within us by the physical food of which we partake. He has said that is one reason why the Bahá'í Feasts make us all so happy. United in love and loving kindness, love is strengthened within us when Bahá'ís eat together.

She makes this special point as to the two birthdays:

He said not a word about His own birthday! He spoke only of the Báb, His mission and message. (He was born during the night of the Báb's Declaration, 22 May 1844).

Florence speaks often of the Master's bountiful table, and of the food served her in 'Akká. She was given such things as coffee scented with rose water, and a peahen's egg.

One noon I apologized (<u>Kh</u>án translating) to 'Abdu'l-Bahá for eating so much. He replied, *"Qurratu'l-'Ayn always ate a great deal. She had little dishes of candy, or fruits and nuts beside her, of which she continually partook."* He then heaped up her plate, saying that as a nursing mother she needed plenty of food, and adding: *"Rice is good. It makes more milk."*

The Gift of Health

The Master continually healed the sick. He often instructed physicians. Ramona Allen Brown tells how, in California, He instructed and carried on medical conversations with her father, a well-known Bay Area physician. He often spoke of what is now called psychosomatic medicine (and indeed He describes in *Some Answered Questions* four types of healing by spiritual means). To a physician he wrote:

> The powers of the sympathetic nerve are neither entirely physical nor spiritual, but are between the two.* The nerve is connected with both. Its phenomena shall be perfect when its spiritual and physical relations are normal. When the material world and

---

* Answer to question of a physician regarding the sympathetic nervous system of the human organism.

the divine world are well co-related, when the hearts become heavenly and the aspirations grow pure and divine, perfect connection shall take place.[1]

In *Memorials of the Faithful,* He tells how a believer maintained his health and peace through contentment:

He spent his days in utter bliss. Here, too, he carried on a small business, which occupied him from morning till noon. In the afternoons he would take his samovar, wrap it in a dark-colored pouch made from a saddlebag, and go off somewhere to a garden or meadow, or out in a field, and have his tea. Sometimes he would be found at the farm of Mazra'ih, or again in the Riḍván Garden; or, at the Mansion, he would have the honor of attending upon Bahá'u'lláh.

[He] . . . would carefully consider every blessing that came his way. "How delicious my tea is today," he would comment. "What perfume, what color! How lovely this meadow is, and the flowers so bright!" He used to say that everything, even air and water, had its own special fragrance. For him the days passed in indescribable delight. Even kings were not so happy as this old man, the people said.[2]

'Abdu'l-Bahá believes in healing through pleasant foods, by the use of simple medicines and of hot or cold water. He says that *"in reality both health and sickness are contagious,"* but the contagion of health *"is exceedingly slow and weak."*[3] He also teaches that a great gain in health will be made by obedience to the Bahá'í law, which discourages tobacco and forbids alcohol.

Unity, prayer, kindness, and service are definite health factors in any society. Jealousy and anger are to be fled, Bahá'u'lláh says, as one would run from a lion.[4] He tells us to avoid hatred deliberately: *"In the garden of thy heart plant naught but the rose of love, . . ."*[5] and the Master says:

Know ye the value of these passing days and vanishing nights. Strive to attain a station of absolute love one toward another. By the absence of love, enmity increases. By the exercise of love, love strengthens and enmities dwindle away.[6]

Love is the source of all the bestowals of God. Until love takes possession of the heart, no other Divine bounty can be revealed in it.[7]

Never become angry with one another. Let your eyes be directed toward the kingdom of truth and not toward the world of creation. Love the creatures for the sake of God and not for themselves. You will never become angry or impatient if you love them for the sake of God. Humanity is not perfect. There are imperfections in every human being, and you will always become unhappy if you look toward the people themselves. But if you look toward God, you will love them and be kind to them, for the world of God is the world of perfection and complete mercy. Therefore, do not look at the shortcomings of anybody; see with the sight of forgiveness. The imperfect eye beholds imperfections. . . . You must love and be kind to everybody, care for the poor, protect the weak, heal the sick, teach and educate the ignorant.[8]

Continence, monogamy, moderation, discipline, hard work, are other health factors, as is the annual nineteen-day daytime fast, which tend to promote the vigor and longevity of Bahá'ís. 'Abdu'l-Bahá's teachings on healing with foods and other simple means are sometimes misinterpreted as endorsements of various health fads; on the contrary, Bahá'u'lláh, says that when ill, Bahá'ís should consult the *"most skilled"* (ádhiq) physician; these "simple" methods are based on depths of knowledge and intuition which will characterize the highly-trained, great doctors of the future. In this connection it is interesting to note how the growing complexity of our modern healing agencies never outdistances modern illness; nor our ever-increasing criminology, the always-gaining rate of crime.

Of that personal purity and cleanliness, which is still so rare in many parts of the world, 'Abdu'l-Bahá was the prime example, and it too is obviously conducive to health. Florence Khánum writes that He was

> dazzlingly, spotlessly . . . shining, from snowy turban-cloth, to white, snowy hair falling upon His shoulders, to white snowy beard and long snowy garment. . . . Although it was high noon, in summer . . . His attire was crisp and fresh-looking, as though He had not been visiting the sick, and in prison, and toiling for mankind since early morning. Often a deliciously fresh rose was tucked in His belt.

In the days before he became Guardian, when 'Abdu'l-Bahá was still on earth, he who was to become the beloved Guardian visited Paris. While there he gave to Florence Khánum and 'Ali-Kuli Khán a soft grey coat of the Master's, which he said the Master had often worn. One night it hung in the present writer's room, when it was to be brushed and refolded in the Persian raw silk cloth that Shoghi Effendi had wrapped it in when he brought it. (This coat, in the same raw silk wrapping, is now in the Bahá'í Temple at Wilmette.) All night I was conscious of its fragrance, even after the many long years since the Master had worn it. The smell of Jacob's raiment is mentioned in the Bible; it was "as the smell of a field which the Lord hath blessed."[9] In Western languages, we speak of the "odor of sanctity," and the phrase is not idle.

Death, the Welcome Messenger

'Abdu'l-Bahá's most vital teaching about health is perhaps what He tells us about death, since innumerable ailments are caused or aggravated by fear of it: The soul is not in the body, it *". . . is connected with the body as the sun is with the mirror."*[1] *"[T]he inner and essential reality of man is not composed of elements and, therefore, cannot be decomposed."*[2] *"If the spirit of man belonged to the elemental existence, the eye could see it, the ear hear it, the hand touch* [it].*"*[3] *"Through his ignorance man fears death; but the death he shrinks from is imaginary. . . ."*[4] *"The spirit or human soul, is the rider, and the body is only the steed."*[5] *"This human body is purely animal in type and, like the animal, it is subject only to the grosser sensibilities. It is utterly bereft of ideation or intellection, utterly incapable of the processes of reason. The animal perceives what its eye sees and judges what the ear hears."* [6] *"The spirit can conduct its affairs without the body. In the world of dreams it is precisely as this light without the chimney glass. It can shine without the glass."* [7]

The Master makes many references to dreams, those mysterious phenomena so little understood by current science and not at all by the average modern man. For Bahá'u'lláh has written in the Seven Valleys that God has deposited this sign in man so that philosophers shall not deny the life beyond or disdain what has been promised them. One day in New York the Master said:

I have made you wait awhile, but as I was tired, I slept. While I was sleeping, I was conversing with you as though speaking at the top of my voice. Then through the effect of my own voice I awoke. As I awoke, one word was upon my lips—the word "imtíyáz" ("distinction"). So I will speak to you upon that subject this morning. [8]

He then proceeded to give His famous talk on distinction:

I desire distinction for you. The Bahá'ís must be distinguished from others of humanity. [9]

He explained that He did not mean financial distinction, nor scientific, nor commercial, nor industrial distinction.

For you I desire spiritual distinction—that is, you must become eminent and distinguished in morals. In the love of God you must become distinguished from all else. You must become distinguished for loving humanity, for unity and accord, for love and justice. In brief, you must become distinguished in all the virtues of the human world—for faithfulness and sincerity, . . . for firmness and steadfastness, for philanthropic deeds and service to the human world, for love toward every human being, . . . for removing prejudices and promoting international peace. Finally, you must become distinguished for heavenly illumination and for acquiring the bestowals of God. I desire this distinction for you.[10]

This dangerous journey of the soul, which we call life, is necessary.

The rational soul is endowed from the beginning with individuality; it does not acquire it through the intermediary of the body. At most, what can be said is that the individuality and identity of the rational soul may be strengthened in this world, and that the soul may either progress and attain to the degrees of perfection or remain in the lowest abyss of ignorance and be veiled from and deprived of beholding the signs of God.[11]

The wisdom of the appearance of the spirit in the body is this: The human spirit is a divine trust which must traverse every degree, for traversing and passing through the degrees of existence is the means of its acquiring perfections. So, for example, when a man travels in an orderly and methodical manner through many different countries and regions, this will most certainly be the means of acquiring perfections, for he will see at first hand various sites, scenes, and regions; learn about the affairs and circumstances of other nations; become familiar with the geography of other lands; acquaint himself with their arts and wonders; become informed of the customs, conduct, and character of their inhabitants; witness the civilization and the advancements of the time; and be apprised of the manner of government, the capacity, and the receptivity of each country. In the same way, when the human spirit traverses the degrees of existence and attains each degree and station—even that of the body—it will assuredly acquire perfections. . . .

. . . Likewise, were the perfections of the spirit not to appear in this world, it would become dark and wholly animalistic.[12]

Man must know that he will always be:

The conception of annihilation is a factor in human degradation . . .[13]

[A]nd existence can never become non-existence. This would be equivalent to saying that light can become darkness . . .[14]

[I]t behooves man to abandon thoughts of non-existence and death, which are absolutely imaginary, and see himself ever-living . . . If he dwells upon the thought of non-existence, he will become utterly incompetent; with weakened willpower his ambition for progress will be lessened and the acquisition of human virtues will cease.[15]

At first it is very difficult to welcome death, but after attaining its new condition the soul is grateful, for it has been released from the bondage of the limited, to enjoy the liberties of the unlimited.[16]

Science, a Pathway to God

The permanence of science, the fact that it belongs to the next world, not this, gives intellectual activities the highest rank; indeed, Bahá'u'lláh makes teachers one of the seven classes of heirs to whom Bahá'ís are recommended to leave their property.

The virtues of humanity are many, but science is the most noble of them all. . . . It is a bestowal of God; it is not material; it is divine. Science is an effulgence of the Sun of Reality, the power of investigating and discovering the verities of the universe, the means by which man finds a pathway to God. All the powers and attributes of man are human and hereditary in origin—outcomes of nature's processes—except the intellect, which is supernatural. . . .

. . . God has . . . deposited this love of reality in man. The development and progress of a nation is according to the measure and degree of that nation's scientific attainments. Through this means its greatness is continually increased, and day by day the welfare and prosperity of its people are assured.

. . . this power of intellectual investigation and research . . . is an eternal gift producing fruits of unending delight. . . . All other blessings are temporary; this is an everlasting possession. . . . it is an eternal blessing and divine bestowal, the supreme gift of God to man. Therefore, you should put forward your most earnest efforts toward the acquisition of science and arts. . . . The man of science is perceiving and endowed with vision, whereas he who is ignorant and neglectful of this development is blind. The investigating mind is attentive, alive; the callous and indifferent mind is deaf and dead. A scientific man is a true index and representative of humanity, for through processes of inductive reasoning and research he is informed of all that appertains to humanity, its status, conditions and happenings. He studies the human body politic, understands social problems and weaves the web and texture of civilization. . . .

. . . science or the attribute of scientific penetration is supernatural and that all other blessings of God are within the boundary of nature. What is the

proof of this? All created things except man are captives of nature. . . .

How shall we utilize these gifts and expend these
bounties? By directing our efforts toward the unifi-
cation of the human race.[1]

Addressing Stanford, one of the great universities of the
West, 'Abdu'l-Bahá said:

The dominion of kings has an ending . . . but the
sovereignty of science is everlasting and without end.
. . . The Greek and Roman kingdoms with all their
grandeur passed away; the ancient sovereignties of
the Orient are but memories, whereas the power and
influence of Plato and Aristotle still continue.[2]

Men and Women
are Equal

In Judaism, Christianity, Islam, sex equality does not exist. The Old Testament says (of the man, to the woman): "He shall rule over thee."[1] And the New Testament: "let the woman learn in silence with all subjection. But I suffer not a woman to teach, nor to usurp authority over the man, but to be in silence."[2] "Wives, submit yourselves unto your own husbands, as unto the Lord."[3] Of men and women the Qur'án, which however gives women a higher place than did previous Faiths, says: "Men are a degree above them."[4]

Obviously, men would like this state of affairs to continue, since it is greatly to their advantage. Today, for example, many an American man, terrified of the growing power of the American woman, has turned to Japan for a wife, because Japanese women are traditionally reared with the object of waiting on their men. Thanks to male opinion and the human propensity for blind imitation, women's role in most parts of the world is still limited to "church, kitchen, and children," but social evolution is catching up, and man today is the ex-lord of creation.

The Master says,

> God does not inquire, "Art thou woman or art thou man?" He judges human actions.[5]

> Science is praiseworthy—whether investigated by the intellect of man or woman.[6]

> [T]he education of woman is more necessary and important than that of man, for woman is the trainer of the child from its infancy. If she be defective and imperfect herself, the child will necessarily be deficient; therefore, imperfection of woman implies a condition of imperfection in all mankind. . . .[7]

He affirms that many a woman has proved superior to men:

> Victoria, Queen of England, was really superior to all the kings of Europe in ability, justness and equitable administration. During her long and brilliant reign the British Empire was immensely extended and enriched, due to her political sagacity, skill and foresight.[8]

Although Ṭáhirih had unveiled and had died for it, becoming "the first woman suffrage martyr,"[9] the actual public emancipation of Persia's women from the veil was slow. Eighty-seven years went by between the Conference at Badasht (1848) where Ṭáhirih had proclaimed woman's equality with man, and the Government's decree that the women of Írán should put aside their veils. Emancipated as to their Bahá'í activities, the Bahá'í women of Persia purposely did not, as a group, unveil in the streets of Persia until it became law to do so; their unveiling would have delayed the event, since one of the reaction's strongest weapons was to emphasize that freedom for women was a Bahá'í idea.

The veil was not a piece of cloth, it was an entire social system. The Bahá'í way replaced the Muslim at an early stage, and Florence Khánum's being invited by the Master (in 1906) to sit at table with His Eastern men guests, although she was a Persian's wife, was one symbol of this. It was however His wish that at that time, in the Holy Land and Persia, she should veil. Her book shows clearly that hostile Muslims were by no means her only enemies; another group was opposed to her for coming out of the West and living as a Persian among Persians; these were the Christian missionaries; partly because they looked down on Persians; and partly, Florence Khánum says, "because of their own lack of success."

The Persian street-veil or chádur, usually of black satin or silk or cotton, enveloped a woman completely, like a tent; the word means tent. The face was covered by a separate, adjustable square of horsehair or (in Turkey) black, silken material, and the veil itself was clutched under the chin in one concealed hand. The garment was not unattractive when worn by Easterners, but was so alien to Western psychology that no Westerner looked right in one. She writes:

> I was given a <u>ch</u>ádur, and taught how to wear it. . . .
> For a young, athletic American woman to so dress
> . . . was, naturally, a hardship. I never wore this dress
> gracefully, and always felt clumsy in it and usually
> exasperated as well. However, it was an adventure,
> and naturally I accepted the ordeal in good grace . . .
> at all events, it was not too much a price to pay, for
> the pleasurable hours with Eastern women it enabled
> me to enjoy . . . *once* it was the cause of happiness.
> . . . The time at 'Akká when I was glad to be in
> <u>ch</u>ádur and veiled, occurred one afternoon, as I was
> hurrying across the large, open prison-courtyard to
> join the ladies outside, for a drive to Bahjí. <u>Kh</u>án
> had taken Raḥím outside, and was waiting near the
> Master's beach wagon, to give Raḥím to me for the
> drive. Suddenly I heard the Master's voice ring out
> commandingly, "<u>Kh</u>án!" Peering through my black
> veil, I glanced all around, but saw not a soul at the
> windows above, nor in the empty courtyard. "Oh

dear!" said I to myself, "the Master wants <u>Kh</u>án and <u>Kh</u>án is not here. Whatever shall I do?" I thought, "the only thing to do is to hurry faster, and to send <u>Kh</u>án back to 'Abdu'l-Bahá." So, clumsily (as usual) I clutched a handful of <u>ch</u>ádur and with veil still down (I had been instructed not to raise the veil if men were about) I hurried on. Again came the Master's loud command in a ringing voice, "<u>Kh</u>án!" "Oh dear," I thought, "the Master must need <u>Kh</u>án immediately!" And peering again around most carefully, through the obscuring veil, still I saw no sign of life anywhere! I hurried forward. For the third time, the Master's voice rang out commandingly, "<u>Kh</u>án!" In desperation, I stopped—and this time raising my veil, I saw the Master standing at the head of the long flight of stone steps leading to His quarters. . . . "<u>Kh</u>án?" I queried, and struggling for a few words in Persian, I replied: "<u>Kh</u>án . . . míyáyand! <u>Kh</u>án is coming." The Master saw it was I and replied, "Oh, <u>Kh</u>ánum, Bifarmá'íd!" (proceed, continue). I then almost ran outside to <u>Kh</u>án and breathlessly told him to go at once to the Master, Who was calling him.

In the evening when we returned from the beautiful drive, <u>Kh</u>án came to listen to the story of the afternoon's experiences. "I must tell you," he said, smiling, "that I found the Master, standing at the head of the steps and leaning against the wall, laughing heartily." "Why, what was it?" I asked. <u>Kh</u>án answered, "The Master wanted me to come to Him, and seeing, He said, apparently a woman of the household hurrying across the courtyard, He called for me. He said He called several times, wondering why the woman did not answer. Finally, He said, "The woman stopped, and turning, raised her veil. I saw it was <u>Kh</u>ánum. . . ." <u>Kh</u>án said he had hardly ever heard the Master laugh so long, and so heartily. "<u>Kh</u>ánum," continued the Master, "wearing the <u>ch</u>ádur and veil, like an old man with a beard too long for him, and not knowing what to do with it."

My father then told her to be happy, that there was a saying among the Persians that whoever brings laughter to one of the Holy Ones is greatly blessed.

The Struggle
for the Tomb

Among woman's great functions will be the abolition of war. 'Abdu'l-Bahá says:

> War and its ravages have blighted the world; the education of woman will be a mighty step toward its abolition . . . for she will use her whole influence against war. . . . She will refuse to give her sons for sacrifice upon the field of battle. In truth, she will be the greatest factor in establishing universal peace and international arbitration. Assuredly, woman will abolish warfare among mankind.[1]

Of war He said,

If a man steals one dollar, he is called a thief and put into prison; if he rapes and pillages an innocent country by military invasion, he is crowned a hero.

How ignorant is humankind! Ferocity does not belong to the kingdom of man. It is the province of man to confer life, not death.[2]

We are all human . . . and all come from Mr Adam's family. Why, then, all these fallacious national and racial distinctions? These boundary lines and artificial barriers have been created by despots and conquerors who sought to attain dominion over mankind, thereby engendering patriotic feeling and rousing selfish devotion to merely local standards of government. As a rule they themselves enjoyed luxuries in palaces, surrounded by conditions of ease and affluence, while armies of soldiers, civilians and tillers of the soil fought and died at their command . . . shedding their innocent blood for a delusion such as "we are Germans," "our enemies are French," etc., when, in reality, all are humankind, all belong to the one family and posterity of Adam, the original father. . . .

God created one earth and one mankind to people it. Man has no other habitation, but man himself has come forth and proclaimed imaginary boundary lines and territorial restrictions. . . .[3]

And He asks this:

We live upon this earth for a few days and then rest beneath it forever. . . . Shall man fight for the tomb which devours him, for his eternal sepulcher? What ignorance could be greater than this? To fight over his grave, to kill another for his grave![4]

He particularly called upon the United States of America to lead the way to world peace, and He warned, on 12 May 1912: *"Just now Europe is a battlefield of ammunition ready for a spark; and one spark will set aflame the whole world."*[5] *"Before these . . . cataclysmic events happen, take the step to prevent it."*[6]

The Master continually stressed the need of a world auxiliary language in the building of peace. He says,

. . . the function of language is to portray the mysteries and secrets of human hearts. The heart is like a box, and language is the key.[7]

He emphasizes that Bahá'u'lláh has not named the universal language, saying that it will be either an existing language or a new one. He himself wrote, however,

The Persian language shall become noteworthy in this cycle; nay, rather, the people shall study it in all the world.[8]

And again:

> . . . regarding the universal language: Ere long significant and scientific discussions concerning this matter will arise among the people of discernment and insight and it will produce the desired result.[9]

God, the Unknowable

Man was created by the conscious will of God. The proof that God is not a blind force is that man is not a blind force. *"Man the creature, has volition . . ."*[1] and his Creator is not less than he. The universe has always existed, because God has always existed; *"this endless universe, likewise has no beginning"*;[2] God's name or attribute the Creator presupposes creation. *"[T]he existence of phenomena implies composition. . . ."*[3] That composition of elements which constitutes life is demonstrably *"neither accidental nor involuntary"*[4]—if it were accidental, it would be an effect without a cause; if it were involuntary, and the elements came together because it was their nature to do so, *"then it would be impossible for a composite being . . . to be decomposed. . . ."*[5] The only remaining possibility is that the process is voluntary, *"which means that composition is effected through a superior will . . . through the eternal Will, the Will of the Living, Eternal, and Self-Subsistent. . . ."*[6]

Having created the world and all that liveth and moveth therein, He, through the direct operation of His unconstrained and sovereign Will, chose to confer upon man the unique distinction and capacity to know Him and to love Him—a capacity that must needs be regarded as the generating impulse and the primary purpose underlying the whole of creation. . . .[7]

And since there can be no tie of direct intercourse to bind the one true God with His creation, and no resemblance whatever can exist between the transient and the Eternal, the contingent and the Absolute, He hath ordained that in every age and dispensation a pure and stainless Soul be made manifest in the kingdoms of earth and heaven.[8]

The Manifestation of God is qualitatively different from man, even such a man as Plato or Leonardo da Vinci: man possesses only two stations or conditions, body and soul; the Manifestation possesses three: body, soul, and the Holy Spirit.[9]

'Abdu'l-Bahá teaches that,

The worlds of God are in perfect harmony and correspondence one with another. Each world in this limitless universe, is as it were, a mirror reflecting the history and nature of all the rest. The physical universe is, likewise, in perfect correspondence with the spiritual or divine realm. The world of matter is an outer expression or facsimile of the inner Kingdom of spirit.[10]

The earthly realm is the mirror of the heavenly Kingdom, and the material world is in accordance with the spiritual world.[11]

Evidently, then, we tend to see things upside down, and what we think is the reality is really the symbol: eyes are the symbol—insight the reality; a lamp is the symbol, and guidance the reality. The sun in the sky is often used by the Master as a symbol of the Manifestation of God, the Sun of Truth. The Manifestation is like the sun, *"which, by virtue of its inherent disposition, must inevitably produce light."* He is *"luminous in Himself,"* while all other souls must borrow light from Him.[12] He is a mirror, blazing with the light of the sun.[13]

In the inner world . . . the Sun of Reality is the Trainer. . . .[14]

When the phenomenal sun appears from the vernal point of dawning in the zodiac, a wondrous and vibrant commotion is set up in the body of the earthly world. The withered trees are quickened with animation, the black soil becomes verdant with new growth, fresh and fragrant flowers bloom, the world of dust is refreshed, renewed life forces surge through the veins of every animate being, and a new springtime carpets the meadows, plains, mountains and valleys with wondrous forms of life. That which was dead and desolate is revived and resuscitated; that which was withered, faded and stricken is transformed by the spirit of a new creation. In the same way the Sun of Reality, when it illumines the horizon of the inner world, animates, vivifies and quickens with a divine and wonderful power.[15]

The Master writes again:

The station of Bahá'u'lláh's Revelation, on the other hand, is represented by the sign Leo, the sun's mid-summer and highest station. By this is meant that this holy Dispensation is illumined with the light of the Sun of Truth shining from its most exalted station, and in the plenitude of its resplendency, its heat and glory.[16]

The Coming of
the Glory

It was only for one purpose that 'Abdu'l-Bahá traveled to the West, to herald the rise of the Sun of Truth:

> Indifferent to the sights and curiosities which habitually invite the attention of travelers and which the members of His entourage often wished Him to visit; careless alike of His comfort and His health; expending every ounce of His energy day after day from dawn till late at night; consistently refusing any gifts or contributions towards the expenses of His travels; unfailing in His solicitude for the sick, the sorrowful and the down-trodden; uncompromising in His championship of the underprivileged races and classes; bountiful as the rain in His generosity to the poor; contemptuous of the attacks launched against Him by vigilant and fanatical exponents of orthodoxy and sectarianism; marvelous in His

frankness while demonstrating, from platform and pulpit, the prophetic Mission of Jesus Christ to the Jews, of the Divine origin of Islam in churches and synagogues, or the truth of Divine Revelation and the necessity of religion to materialists, atheists or agnostics; unequivocal in His glorification of Bahá'u'lláh at all times and within the sanctuaries of divers sects and denominations; adamant in His refusal, on several occasions, to curry the favor of people of title and wealth both in England and in the United States; and last but not least incomparable in the spontaneity, the genuineness and warmth of His sympathy and loving-kindness shown to friend and stranger alike, believer and unbeliever, rich and poor, high and low, whom He met, either intimately or casually, whether on board ship, or whilst pacing the streets, in parks or public squares, at receptions or banquets, in slums or mansions, in the gatherings of His followers or the assemblage of the learned, He, the incarnation of every Bahá'í virtue and the embodiment of every Bahá'í ideal, continued for three crowded years to trumpet to a world sunk in materialism and already in the shadow of war, the healing, the God-given truths enshrined in His Father's Revelation.[1]

"I belong to him that loveth Me, that holdeth fast My commandments . . ." Bahá'u'lláh has written.[2] Above all, He

belonged to 'Abdu'l-Bahá. Lingeringly, the Master would tell of His Father:

> . . . all the contemporaneous religious sects and systems rose against Him. His enemies were kings. . . . These kings represented some fifty million people, all of whom under their influence and domination were opposed to Bahá'u'lláh. Therefore, in effect Bahá'u'lláh, singly and alone, virtually withstood fifty million enemies. . . . Although they were determined upon extinguishing the light in that most brilliant lantern, . . . day by day His splendor became more radiant. . . . Surrounded by enemies who were seeking His life, He never sought to conceal Himself, did nothing to protect Himself; on the contrary, in His spiritual might and power He was at all times visible before the faces of men, easy of access, serenely withstanding the multitudes who were opposing Him.[3]

While addressing these powerful kings and rulers He was a prisoner in a Turkish dungeon. Consider how marvelous it was for a prisoner under the eye and control of the Turks to arraign so boldly and severely the very king who was responsible for His imprisonment. What power this is! What greatness! . . . and so constant and firm was He that He caused their banners to come down and His own standard to be upraised. . . . Consider what a mighty power this is![4]

Again, the Master told how even Bahá'u'lláh's enemies praised Him; He was, they said, "truly great; his influence was mighty and wonderful. This personage was glorious; his power was tremendous, his speech most eloquent . . ." Then they would add: What a pity that He was a "misleader of the people."[5] Some wrote satiric poems about Him, since in any case, having encountered Him, they could not let Him alone: they had to do something about Him. And even these poems turned out to be praise. One wrote:

Beware! lest ye approach this person, for he is possessed of such power and of such an eloquent tongue that he is a sorcerer. He charms men, He drugs them; He is a hypnotizer. Beware! Beware! lest you read his book[,] follow his example and associate with his companions because they are possessors of tremendous power and they are misleaders.[6]

These warnings influenced many in His favor.

The more His enemies wrote against Him, the more the people were attracted and the greater the number who came to inquire about the truth. They would say "This is remarkable. This is a great man, and we must investigate. We must look into this cause to find out what it all means, to discover its purpose, examine its proofs. . . ." In Persia the mullás went so far as to proclaim from the pulpits against the Cause of Bahá'u'lláh casting their turbans upon the ground—a sign of great agitation—and crying out, "O people! This Bahá'u'lláh is a sorcerer. . . .[7]

The Master said of His Father's forty years' imprisonment,

Observe how rarely human souls sacrifice their pleasure or comfort for others. . . . Yet all the divine Manifestations suffered, offered Their lives and blood, sacrificed Their . . . comfort and all They possessed for the sake of mankind. Therefore, consider how much They love.[8]

The struggle between good and evil will always go on, because it is inherent in the human situation: man is a reality standing between darkness and light.[9] But it will now be conducted on a far higher level, with millions of human beings consciously, deliberately working for good. Up to now many a person has tried to reform other people (the usual method was to go and live with the underprivileged—in that way, one had a head start); from now on many a person will try to reform himself; not in a cave or desert but in his relationships with other people. He had little hope of doing this in a material world, since, under materialism, *"good and evil advance together and maintain the same pace."*[10] Now the good is aided by a mighty spiritual plus.

Man is perfectible, but not perfection; only God is perfection.[11] The human perfectibility which 'Abdu'l-Bahá teaches is not a vision but a simple truth; the World Order of Bahá'u'lláh is not a utopia; most human lives are ineffective today and the world is inevitably going to be coordinated so that they can become effective; so that each human being can *"become expressive . . . of all the bounties of life to mankind."*[12] People who think this is a utopia would be amazed to find how methodically it is being established in the world. 'Abdu'l-Bahá has "categorically asserted that the 'banner of the unity of' mankind would be hoisted, that the tabernacle of universal peace would be raised and the world become another world.'"[13]

He Himself was the most methodical of beings. He said:

In this world we judge a cause or movement by its progress and development. Some movements appear, manifest a brief period of activity, then discontinue. Others show forth a greater measure of growth and strength, but before attaining mature development, weaken, disintegrate and are lost in oblivion. . . .

There is still another kind of movement or cause which from a very small, inconspicuous beginning goes forward with sure and steady progress, gradually broadening and widening until it has assumed universal dimensions. The Bahá'í Movement is of this nature. For instance, when Bahá'u'lláh was exiled from Persia with 'Abdu'l-Bahá and the rest of His family, they travelled the long road from Ṭihrán to Baghdád, passing through many towns and villages. During the whole of that journey and distance they did not meet a single believer in the Cause for which they had been banished. At that time very little was known about it in any part of the world. Even in Baghdád there was but one believer who had been taught by Bahá'u'lláh Himself in Persia. Later on, two or three others appeared. You will see, therefore, that at the beginning the Cause of Bahá'u'lláh was almost unknown, but on account of being a divine Movement it grew and developed with irresistible spiritual power. . . .[14]

Today,

The number of territories included within the pale of the Faith, embracing all the sovereign states and chief dependencies of the planet, has . . . in consequence of this prodigious effort [the global Crusade] been raised to two hundred and fifty–one. . . .[15]

One day in the United States He told this story:

Many years ago in Baghdád I saw a certain officer sitting upon the ground. Before him a large paper was placed into which he was sticking needles tipped with small red and white flags. First he would stick them into the paper, then thoughtfully pull them out and change their position. I watched him with curious interest for a long time, then asked, "What are you doing?" He replied, "I have in mind something which is historically related of Napoleon I during his war against Austria. One day, it is said, his secretary found him sitting upon the ground as I am now doing, sticking needles into a paper before him. His secretary inquired what it meant. Napoleon answered, 'I am on the battlefield figuring out my next victory. You see, Italy and Austria are defeated, and France is triumphant.' In the great campaign which followed, everything came out just as he said. His army carried his plans to a complete success. Now, I am doing the same as Napoleon, figuring out a great campaign of military conquest." I said, "Where is your army? Napoleon had an army already equipped when he figured out his victory. You have no army. Your forces exist only on paper. You have no power to conquer countries. First get ready your army, then sit upon the ground with your needles."[16]

People ask: Why, if He was so wonderful, did He have so many enemies? The answer is, because He was so wonderful. Florence Khánum relates that one day she and 'Alí-Kuli Khán were alone with the Master and He was conversing with them. Suddenly, powerfully, with His two clenched fists, the Master beat upon His breast. And then with great vigor and emphasis: *"'Abdu'l-Bahá has many enemies!"* He exclaimed. *"Let there be more! 'Abdu'l-Bahá is equal to all of them!"*

Articles against the Faith He called *"the harmless twittering of sparrows." "Rest ye in the assurance of firmness."*[17] *"They will spread the Message."*[18]

All who stand up in the cause of God will be persecuted and misunderstood. It hath ever been so, and will ever be. Let neither enemy nor friend disturb your composure, destroy your happiness, deter your accomplishment. Rely wholly upon God. . . .

. . . Let nothing defeat you. God is your helper. . . . Be firm in the Heavenly Covenant. Pray for strength. It will be given to you, no matter how difficult the conditions.[19]

When he ['Abdu'l-Bahá] arrived in 'Akká they placed chains upon his limbs and circlets of steel were locked around his ankles and knees. While the guards were doing this 'Abdu'l-Bahá laughed and sang. They were astonished and said, "How is this? . .

. When prisoners are ironed in this way, they usually cry out, weep and lament." 'Abdu'l-Bahá replied, "I rejoice because you are doing me a great kindness. . . . For a long time I have wished to know the feelings of a prisoner in irons, to experience what other men have been subjected to. I have heard of this; now you have taught me what it is. You have given me this opportunity. Therefore I sing and am very happy. I am very thankful to you." After a time the men who had been appointed to keep guard over me became as loving brothers and companions. They strove to lighten my imprisonment by acts of kindness. They said, "In order that you may not be subjected to the jeers of the people when you walk upon the streets we will arrange your clothing so these chains are not visible." They took the chains which were upon my limbs, gathered the ends together and wrapped them as a girdle around my waist, then arranged my clothing so no chains were visible. One day I wished to go to the hamman (public bath). The guards said, "It will not be possible for you to go to the bath unless these chains are removed; and furthermore it will attract notice from the people in the streets." 'Abdu'l-Bahá said, "I will go."

The guards then carefully gathered the hanging chains around my waist, covered them with my clothing and we went forth. As we passed through the streets, 'Abdu'l-Bahá took the chains from his waist, flung their loose, dangling ends over his shoulders in full view and walked to the hamman, followed by a great crowd of hooting, jeering people. The guards were most unhappy, but 'Abdu'l-Bahá was in supreme joy because of this opportunity to walk in the freedom of the Pathway of God.[20]

Because the Master is inseparable from His teachings, we have tried in the foregoing to indicate some of the main lines of the vast body of His work. We have tried to hint at His teaching methods, since He is above all the great Teacher, making reality come alive, instead of lying in the death of the abstraction. Often He taught by indicating some person sitting near Him, or some object that was there. For example, explaining the animal spirit, which is the second category of the five into which spirit is divided, He said: *"It may be likened to this lamp: When oil, wick, and flame are brought together and combined, it is lit. . . ."*[21] And you think of the lamplight falling across the table; you wonder why that particular lamp was given immortality. You remember being told in the Master's household that He was very particular that guests should always be honored (He even placed this injunction in one of the most solemn and tender of all Bahá'í prayers, the prayer revealed by Him for the dead); and that once when there were guests and the lamp chimney was not highly-enough polished, He sent for it to be replaced. And you think of the lamplight falling across the table; you see His face in the lamplight and inevitably you remember what everything on earth makes you remember: that no lamp will ever light up His face any more. You feel, for the thousandth time, that pang of loss that inherent every day in every sunset, and you understand what the Báb meant in telling of the death of a Prophet when He said, *"All sorrow is only the shadow of that sorrow."* [22]

If we had to choose one short sentence summing up His wishes for man, it might be this:

Array yourselves in the perfection of divine virtues. [23]

One day in 'Akká, writes Juliet Thompson in her diary, a pilgrim, looking at a magnificent rose, said: "I wish I might be like this rose and exhale such fragrances." And 'Abdu'l-Bahá, Who often immortally returned some casual remark, answered:

One could be much more beautiful than this rose. For the rose perishes. Its fragrance is just for a time. But no winter has any effect upon such a Rose as Man. [24]

Notes

The Unity of East and West

1. Bahá'u'lláh, *Gleanings from the Writings of Bahá'u'lláh,* no. 77.
2. Shoghi Effendi, *The World Order of Bahá'u'lláh,* p. 131.
3. Shoghi Effendi, *God Passes By,* p. 387.
4. Bahá'u'lláh, quoted in Shoghi Effendi, *The World Order of Bahá'u'lláh,* p. 135.
5. Ibid.
6. Ibid., p. 136.
7. Shoghi Effendi, *God Passes By,* p. 258.
8. Ibid., p. 441.
9. Ibid., p. 442.
10. Ibid., pp. 442–44.
11. Ibid., p. 444.
12. Ibid., p. 489.

13. Qur'án 3:194, 197.

14. 'Abdu'l-Bahá quoted in *Star of the West*, 8 September 1912, Vol. iii:10, p. 16.

15. Shoghi Effendi, *God Passes By*, p. 522.

16. Shoghi Effendi, *The World Order of Bahá'u'lláh*, p. 144.

17. Ibid., p. 147.

18. Shoghi Effendi, *God Passes By*, p. 519.

19. Shoghi Effendi, *The World Order of Bahá'u'lláh*, p. 52.

20. 'Abdu'l-Bahá, *The Promulgation of Universal Peace*, p. 47.

21. Ibid.

22. Ibid.

23. Ibid., p. 47.

The Manuscript of Florence K͟hánum

1. It should be noted that passages taken from the memoirs of the author's mother, Mrs. Florence Breed Khan (referred to herein as Florence K͟hánum), fall into the category of pilgrims' notes. These passages, which describe the words and actions of 'Abdu'l-Bahá, should be considered the recollections of the author, and not as authoritative accounts of the words and deeds of the Master.

The Master in 'Akká

1. 'Abdu'l-Bahá, *The Promulgation of Universal Peace*, p. 259.
2. Ibid., p. 373.
3. Ibid., p. 33.

The Attainable Perfections of Man

1. 'Abdu'l-Bahá, *The Promulgation of Universal Peace*, p. 534.
2. Ibid., p. 5.
3. Ibid., p. 599.
4. Ibid., p. 570.
5. Ibid., p. 657.
6. 'Abdu'l-Bahá, in *Bahá'í Prayers*, p. 31.
7. Bahá'u'lláh, *Gleanings from the Writings of Bahá'u'lláh*, no. 131.3.
8. Bahá'u'lláh, The Hidden Words, Persian, no. 72.
9. 'Abdu'l-Bahá, *Some Answered Questions*, no. 52.
10. Ibid.
11. Ibid., no. 46.4.
12. 'Abdu'l-Bahá, *The Promulgation of Universal Peace*, p. 335.
13. Ibid., pp. 78–80.
14. 'Abdu'l-Bahá, *Some Answered Questions*, no. 36.6.
15. Ibid., no. 25.2
16. Ibid, no. 36.6.
17. Ibid.

18. Ibid., no. 36.8.

19. 'Abdu'l-Bahá, *The Promulgation of Universal Peace*, p. 367.

20. Ibid. p. 93.

21. Ibid., p 416.

22. Ibid., p. 391.

23. Ibid., p. 338.

24. Ibid., p. 421.

25. Ibid., p. 257.

26. Ibid., p. 365.

27. Ibid., pp. 433–34.

28. Qur'án 25:18.

29. Ibid., 59:19.

30. 'Abdu'l-Bahá, *The Promulgation of Universal Peace*, p. 657.

31. Ibid., p. 656.

32. Ibid., p. 654.

33. Ibid., p. 656.

34. Ibid., p. 657,

35. Ibid., pp. 366–67.

36. 'Abdu'l-Bahá, *Some Answered Questions*, no. 50.4.

How to Kill Prejudice

1. 'Abdu'l-Bahá, *The Promulgation of Universal Peace*, p. 94.

Man, the Preoccupied

1. Shoghi Effendi, *The Promised Day is Come*, p. 6.
2. Ibid., p. 3.

The Development of Love

1. 'Abdu'l-Bahá, *The Promulgation of Universal Peace*, p. 104.
2. Ibid., p. 50.
3. Ibid., p. 59.
4. Ibid., pp. 4–5.
5. Ibid., p. 44..
6. Ibid., p. 46.
7. Ibid., p. 63
8. Ibid., p. 66.
9. Ibid., p. 127.
10. Ibid., p. 444.
11. *Time*, 6 May 1957.

Love is Not Enough

1. 'Abdu'l-Bahá, *Selections from the Writings of 'Abdu'l-Bahá*, no. 38.5.
2. 'Abdu'l-Bahá, *The Promulgation of Universal Peace*, p. 99.
3. Ibid., pp. 99–100.

4. 'Abdu'l-Bahá, *Selections from the Writings of 'Abdu'l-Bahá,* no. 44.1.

5. 'Abdu'l-Bahá, *The Promulgation of Universal Peace,* p. 333.

6. 'Abdu'l-Bahá, *Some Answered Questions,* no. 77.6.

7. Ibid., no. 77.8.

8. Ibid., no. 77.10.

9. Ibid.

10. 'Abdu'l-Bahá, *Some Answered Questions,* no. 77.10.

11. *Time,* 8 April 1957.

The Trap of Imitation

1. 'Abdu'l-Bahá, *The Promulgation of Universal Peace,* p. 496.

2. Ibid., p. 38.

3. 'Abdu'l-Bahá, *Some Answered Questions,* no. 55.5–6.

4. 'Abdu'l-Bahá, *The Promulgation of Universal Peace,* p. 323.

5. Ibid., p. 407.

6. Ibid., p. 381.

7. Ibid., p. 633.

8. 'Abdu'l-Bahá, *Some Answered Questions,* no. 66.8.

9. 'Abdu'l-Bahá, *The Promulgation of Universal Peace,* p. 411.

10. 'Abdu'l-Bahá, *Some Answered Questions,* no. 30.5.

11. Ibid., no. 30.8.

12. Ibid., no. 30.9.

13. 'Abdu'l-Bahá, *The Promulgation of Universal Peace,* p. 261.

14. Ibid., pp. 634–35.

15. 'Abdu'l-Bahá, *Some Answered Questions,* no. 67.

16. 'Abdu'l-Bahá, *The Promulgation of Universal Peace,* p. 118.

17. Ibid., pp. 118–19.

18. Ibid., p. 119.

19. Ibid., p. 515.

20. Ibid.

21. See 'Abdu'l-Bahá, *The Promulgation of Universal Peace,* p. 534.

22. Ibid., p. 409.

23. Ibid., p. 406.

24. 'Abdu'l-Bahá, *Some Answered Questions,* no. 81.6.

25. 'Abdu'l-Bahá, *The Promulgation of Universal Peace,* p. 130.

26. Bahá'u'lláh, *Gleanings from the Writings of Bahá'u'lláh,* no. 166.

27. 'Abdu'l-Bahá, *The Promulgation of Universal Peace,* p. 538.

28. 'Abdu'l-Bahá, *Some Answered Questions,* no. 45.

29. 'Abdu'l-Bahá, *The Promulgation of Universal Peace,* p. 520.

30. Ibid.

31. Ibid.

32. Ibid., p. 583.

33. Ibid.; Talk dated 9 November 1912.

34. Ibid., p. 579.

35. Ibid., p. 584.

36. Ibid.

Mankind is One People

1. Acts 17:26.

2. 'Abdu'l-Bahá, *The Promulgation of Universal Peace,* p. 396.

3. Ibid., p. 398.

4. Ibid., p. 493.

5. 'Abdu'l-Bahá, *Some Answered Questions,* no. 81.6.

6. Ibid., no. 81.7.

Show Forth True Economics

1. J. E. Esslemont, *Bahá'u'lláh and the New Era,* p. 188.

2. 'Abdu'l-Bahá, *The Promulgation of Universal Peace,* p. 479.

3. See 'Abdu'l-Bahá, *The Promulgation of Universal Peace,* pp. 44–46.

4. Ibid., p. 335.

5. Ibid., p. 334.

6. Bahá'u'lláh, *Gleanings from the Writings of Bahá'u'lláh,* no. 145.

The Assassin's Prisoner

1. See George Dorys, *The Private Life of the Sultan of Turkey*, 1901.
2. Op. cit., p. 77s.
3. Ibid., pp. 158, 163, 184.
4. Shoghi Effendi, *God Passes By*, p. 420.
5. Ibid.
6. Ibid., p. 427.
7. 'Abdu'l-Bahá, *The Promulgation of Universal Peace*, p. 49.
8. Ibid., p. 314.

'Abdu'l-Bahá's Birthday

1. Ibid., p. 195.

The Gift of Health

1. 'Abdu'l-Bahá, *Tablets of Abdul-Baha Abbas*, vol. ii, p. 309.
2. 'Abdu'l-Bahá, *Memorials of the Faithful*, p. 25.
3. 'Abdu'l-Bahá, *Some Answered Questions*, no. 72.3.
4. J. E. Esslemont, *Bahá'u'lláh and the New Era*, ch. 7.
5. Bahá'u'lláh, The Hidden Words, Persian, no. 3.
6. 'Abdu'l-Bahá, *The Promulgation of Universal Peace*, p. 12.
7. Ibid., p. 20.
8. Ibid., p. 128.
9. Gen. 27:27.

Death, the Welcome Messenger

1. 'Abdu'l-Bahá, *Some Answered Questions,* no. 81.11.

2. 'Abdu'l-Bahá, *The Promulgation of Universal Peace,* p. 585.

3. Ibid., p. 429.

4. Ibid., p. 122.

5. Ibid., p. 587.

6. Ibid.

7. Ibid.

8. Ibid., p. 264.

9. Ibid., p. 265.

10. Ibid., pp. 265–66.

11. 'Abdu'l-Bahá, *Some Answered Questions,* no. 66.4.

12. Ibid., no. 52.2–3.

13. 'Abdu'l-Bahá, *The Promulgation of Universal Peace,* p. 123.

14. Ibid., pp. 120–21.

15. Ibid., p. 123.

16. Ibid., pp. 64–65.

Science, a Pathway to God

1. 'Abdu'l-Bahá, *The Promulgation of Universal Peace,* pp. 66–69.

2. Ibid., p. 493.

Men and Women are Equal

1. Genesis 3:16.
2. I Timothy 2:11–12.
3. Ephesians 5:22.
4. Qur'án 2:228.
5. 'Abdu'l-Bahá, *The Promulgation of Universal Peace,* p. 185.
6. Ibid., p. 392.
7. Ibid., p. 185.
8. Ibid., p. 393.
9. Shoghi Effendi, *God Passes By,* p. 118.

The Struggle for the Tomb

1. 'Abdu'l-Bahá, *The Promulgation of Universal Peace,* pp. 149–50.
2. Ibid., p. 142.
3. Ibid., p. 501.
4. Ibid.
5. Ibid., p. 169.
6. Ibid.
7. Ibid., p. 82.
8. 'Abdu'l-Bahá, *Tablets of Abdul-Baha Abbas,* Vol. ii, p. 306.
9. Ibid., Vol. iii, p. 596.

God the Unknowable

1. 'Abdu'l-Bahá, *The Promulgation of Universal Peace,* p. 113.

2. 'Abdu'l-Bahá, *Some Answered Questions,* no. 47.3.

3. 'Abdu'l-Bahá, *The Promulgation of Universal Peace,* p. 596.

4. Ibid., p. 598.

5. Ibid.

6. Ibid.

7. Bahá'u'lláh, *Gleanings from the Writings of Bahá'u'lláh,* no. 27.2.

8. Ibid., no. 27.4.

9. 'Abdu'l-Bahá, *Some Answered Questions,* no. 38.

10. 'Abdu'l-Bahá, *The Promulgation of Universal Peace,* p. 377.

11. 'Abdu'l-Bahá, *Some Answered Questions,* no. 81.6.

12. Ibid., no. 39.3.

13. See ibid., nos. 39, 54.

14. 'Abdu'l-Bahá, *The Promulgation of Universal Peace,* p. 378.

15. Ibid., pp. 378–79.

16. Shoghi Effendi, *The World Order of Bahá'u'lláh,* p. 127.

The Coming of the Glory

1. Shoghi Effendi, *God Passes By,* pp. 446–47.

2. Bahá'u'lláh, *Epistle to the Son of the Wolf,* p. 25.

3. 'Abdu'l-Bahá, *The Promulgation of Universal Peace,* pp. 234–35.

4. Ibid., p. 609.

5. Ibid., p. 614.

6. Ibid.

7. 'Abdu'l-Bahá, *The Promulgation of Universal Peace,* p. 614.

8. Ibid., p. 359.

9. Ibid., p. 657.

10. Ibid., p. 151.

11. 'Abdu'l-Bahá, *Some Answered Questions,* no. 31.

12. 'Abdu'l-Bahá, *The Promulgation of Universal Peace,* p. 21.

13. Shoghi Effendi, *God Passes By,* p. 446.

14. 'Abdu'l-Bahá, *The Promulgation of Universal Peace,* p. 59.

15. Shoghi Effendi, *Messages to the Bahá'í World, 1950–1957,* p. 105.

16. 'Abdu'l-Bahá, *The Promulgation of Universal Peace,* p. 350–51.

17. Ibid., p. 604.

18. Ibid., p. 606.

19. 'Abdu'l-Bahá, in *The Compilation of Compilations,* Vol. i (Crisis and victory), pp. 155–6. This is a revised translation of Star of the West, Vol. 4:5 (5 June 1913), p. 88, revised translation.

20. 'Abdu'l-Bahá, in *Star of the West,* Vol. 4:5 (5 June 1913), p. 88.

21. 'Abdu'l-Bahá, *Some Answered Questions,* no. 55.4.

22. *Le Bayan Persan,* translated by A. L. M. Nicolas, Vol. ii, p. 118.

23. 'Abdu'l-Bahá, *The Promulgation of Universal Peace,* p. 9.

24. 'Abdu'l-Bahá, quoted in *The Diary of Juliet Thompson,* p. 33.

Bibliography

Works of Bahá'u'lláh

Epistle to the Son of the Wolf. 1st pocket-size ed. Translated by Shoghi Effendi. Wilmette, IL: Bahá'í Publishing Trust, 1988.

Gleanings from the Writings of Bahá'u'lláh. Translated by Shoghi Effendi. Wilmette, IL: Bahá'í Publishing, 2005.

The Hidden Words. Translated by Shoghi Effendi. Wilmette, IL: Bahá'í Publishing, 2002.

Works of 'Abdu'l-Bahá

Memorials of the Faithful. Translated and annotated by Marzieh Gail. Wilmette, IL: Bahá'í Publishing, 1997.

The Promulgation of Universal Peace: Talks Delivered by 'Abdu'l-Bahá during His Visit to the United States and

Canada in 1912. Compiled by Howard MacNutt. 2d ed. Wilmette, IL: Bahá'í Publishing, 2012.

Selections from the Writings of 'Abdu'l-Bahá. Compiled by the Research Department of the Universal House of Justice. Translated by a Committee at the Bahá'í World Center and Marzieh Gail. Wilmette, IL: Bahá'í Publishing, 2010.

Some Answered Questions. Haifa: Bahá'í World Centre, 2014.

Tablets of Abdul-Baha Abbas. 3 vols. New York: Bahai Publishing Society, 1909–16.

Works of Shoghi Effendi

God Passes By. New ed. Wilmette, IL: Bahá'í Publishing Trust, 1974.

Messages to the Bahá'í World, 1950–1957. Wilmette: Bahá'í Publishing Trust, 1971.

The Promised Day Is Come. 1st pocket-size ed. Wilmette, IL: Bahá'í Publishing Trust, 1996.

The World Order of Bahá'u'lláh: Selected Letters. 1st pocket-size ed. Wilmette, IL: Bahá'í Publishing Trust, 1991.

Compilations of Bahá'í Writings

Bahá'í Prayers: A Selection of Prayers Revealed by

Bahá'u'lláh, the Báb, and 'Abdu'l-Bahá. New ed. Wilmette, IL: Bahá'í Publishing Trust, 2002.

The Compilation of Compilations: Prepared by the Universal House of Justice, 1963–1990. 2 vols. Australia: Bahá'í Publications Australia, 1991.

Other Works

Dorys, George. *The Private Life of the Sultan of Turkey.* New York: D. Appleton and Co., 1901.

Esslemont, John E. *Bahá'u'lláh and the New Era.* Wilmette, IL: Bahá'í Publishing, 2010.

Nicolas, A. L. M. (trans.), *Le Bayan Persan.* 4 vols. Paris: 1911–14.

Star of the West. Multiple volumes cited.

Thompson, Juliet. *The Diary of Juliet Thompson: Memoirs of 'Abdu'l-Bahá in the Holy Land, Europe, and America.* Los Angeles: Kalimat Press, 1983.